CONTENTS

INTRODUCTION

This book is organised into eight chapters; at the beginning of many of the chapters is an introduction giving hints and tips related to the subject of the chapter. Inexperienced cooks are advised to read the introduction before beginning a recipe in that chapter.

The basic recipes at the start of each chapter are referred to later in the chapter and elsewhere in the book.

Measurements
All the spoon measures in this book are level unless stated otherwise.
3 tsp = 1 tbsp
8 tbsp = 5 fl oz = 150 ml = ¼ pint

Eggs are taken to be size 2 unless stated otherwise.

When following these recipes please use either the metric measurements or the imperial; do not mix them and all will be well.

When a recipe states '175 g (6 oz) pastry' it means pastry made using 175 g (6 oz) flour. It does not mean 175 g (6 oz) prepared pastry.

Measurements for can sizes are approximate.

American equivalents

	Metric	Imperial	American
Butter, margarine	225 g	8 oz	1 cup
Shredded suet	100 g	4 oz	1 cup
Flour	100 g	4 oz	1 cup
Currants	150 g	5 oz	1 cup
Sugar	200 g	7 oz	1 cup
Syrup	335 g	11½ oz	1 cup

An American pint is 16 fl oz compared with the imperial pint of 20 fl oz. A standard American cup measure is considered to hold 8 fl oz.

THE WI BOOK OF
DFSSERTS

JANET

ε

PRESS

ACKNOWLEDGEMENTS

Illustrated by Vanessa Luff
Edited by Sue Jacquemier and Rosemary Wadey
Designed by Clare Clements
Cover photography by James Jackson

ISBN 0 85223 317 5

Published by Ebury Press
National Magazine House
72 Broadwick Street
London W1V 2BP

First impression 1984

Filmset by
D. P. Media Limited, Hitchin, Hertfordshire

Reproduced, printed and bound in Great Britain by
Hazell Watson & Viney Limited,
Member of the BPCC Group,
Aylesbury, Bucks

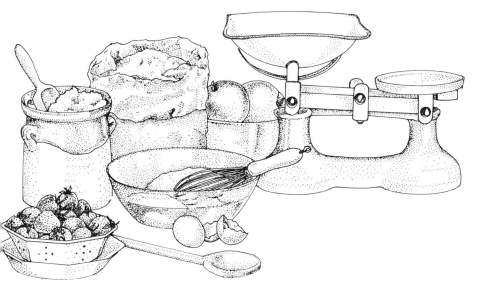

FAMILY PUDDINGS

Several of these recipes are for 'boiled' puddings – traditionally cheap, nourishing and easy, and used by generations of countrywomen to fill a hungry gap. Others are 'steamed' rather than boiled.

It will be useful to know what the terms 'steamed' and 'boiled' mean.

The only puddings in this chapter that are truly 'boiled' are the spotted dick and the roly-poly ones which are literally cooked in boiling water.

The 'steamed' puddings are not these days cooked in a steamer over boiling water; they are put, in their basins, into a closely lidded pan of boiling water. The water should reach half way up the basin and there should be at least an inch between the basin and the edge of the pan so that the steam can circulate. The water should be kept steadily simmering and replenished with boiling water as it evaporates. The recipes state how long the pudding should cook for, but when it is done and out of the pan, let it stand for a minute or two. The pastry will shrink and it will turn out more easily.

Pudding cloths are handy things to have and easily made from an old sheet. They have a string to pull them in and a handle sewn to the top. They are meant for a conventional china pudding basin with a rim – still much the best sort.

The boiled puddings are wrapped in a floured oblong cloth like Tom Kitten and you can hook them out by the strings at the ends.

If the pudding cooked in a basin has sunk, or the roly-poly is soggy, it is because the water has gone off the boil. If a fruit pudding collapses when turned out, it is often because there is not enough filling.

Sauces

Custard powder, of course, makes an easy, economical sauce for family puddings. It is greatly improved by the use of soft, brown sugar instead of white, and an egg yolk beaten into the milk and powder at the mixing stage. The whisked egg white can be folded in when the custard is cool.

Greaseproof paper cut to fit the bowl or jug, dampened and pressed smoothly over the custard, prevents that bane of childhood, the thick skin.

Sweetened, condensed milk, fruit yoghurts, pure fruit juice from a can, and a bar of chocolate melted with the top of the milk, all make quick and easy sauces. All chocolate should be melted in a basin over hot water or in a microwave oven. Evaporated milk will whip if chilled for 24 hours beforehand.

SPONGE PUDDING

Serves 4–6

100 g (4 oz) butter
100 g (4 oz) caster sugar
2 eggs
225 g (8 oz) self-raising flour
50 ml (2 fl oz) milk
3 tbsp jam or golden syrup

Butter a 750-ml (1½-pint) pudding basin. Cream the butter and sugar until pale and fluffy. Beat the eggs and add to the mixture. Beat again. Sieve the flour and fold in with a metal spoon. Add the milk, still folding gently, to make a soft dropping mixture. Add the jam or syrup to the basin, spreading it over the base, then add the sponge mixture, cover with pleated greaseproof paper and a pudding cloth or foil, and steam for 1½ hours.

When ready, turn out onto a serving dish and serve with extra melted jam or syrup as a sauce.

The creaming and then the beating of the butter, sugar and eggs incorporates air which makes the pudding light. The gentle folding in of the flour with a metal spoon makes certain that the air is not knocked out again. Butter really is best for this one.

This is the basic steamed sponge, it is quick to make and pretty well foolproof.

BELVOIR ORANGE PUDDING

Serves 4

2 eggs, separated
grated rind and juice of 2 oranges
100 g (4 oz) butter
200 g (7 oz) caster sugar
100 g (4 oz) fresh white
    breadcrumbs
scant ½ tsp baking powder
2 Cox's orange pippin apples

Butter a 750-ml (1½-pint) basin. Cream the butter and 100 g (4 oz) sugar, add the yolks and beat well. Add the breadcrumbs, the orange rind and juice. Mix lightly and then add the baking powder. Spoon into the basin, cover with pleated greaseproof paper and a pudding cloth or foil and steam for 40 minutes.

Heat the oven to 220°C (425°F) mark 7. Prepare the base. Peel, core and dice the apples. Whisk the egg whites until stiff. Fold in nearly all the remaining sugar and then the diced apple. Spread on a glass ovenproof plate and dust with the remaining sugar. Set the meringue in a hot oven – do this about 10 minutes before the pudding is ready. Turn the pudding out into the middle of the soft meringue and serve. A spoonful or two of orange juice from a can is a good and easy sauce for this fresh, light pudding – which really does call for butter.

GUARD'S PUDDING

Serves 4

200 g (7 oz) fresh brown
    breadcrumbs
175 g (6 oz) shredded suet
100 g (4 oz) dark soft brown sugar
¼ tsp salt
3 tbsp strawberry jam
1 egg (size 1 or 2)
½ tsp bicarbonate of soda

Mix all the dry ingredients together. Beat the jam into the egg with the bicarbonate of soda. Mix well and add to the dry ingredients. Turn into a well greased 750-ml (1½-pint) pudding basin. Cover with a pleated circle of greaseproof paper and a pudding cloth or foil. Steam for 2½ hours. Turn out and serve with custard sauce or crème à la vanille (see page 25).

JAM ROLY-POLY

Serves 4

225 g (8 oz) self-raising flour
½ tsp salt
100 g (4 oz) shredded suet
approx. 150 ml (¼ pint) cold water
4–6 tbsp jam

Sieve the flour and salt into a bowl. Add the suet and mix with sufficient water to give a soft, springy dough. Roll out on a lightly floured board to an oblong 25 x 20 cm (10 x 8 inches). Trim the edges and spread generously up to 1 cm (½ inch) from the edge with jam. Roll up tightly. Wrap loosely in greased greaseproof paper, then in a floured pudding cloth or foil – not too tight, for the roly-poly swells. Tie the ends with string and boil for 2½ to 3 hours.

Variation
For Spotted Dick, spread the rolled out suet pastry with warm golden syrup, sprinkle mixed dried fruit liberally over this and proceed as for jam roly-poly.

PINEAPPLE UPSIDE-DOWN PUDDING

Serves 4–5

2 tbsp clear honey
4 pineapple slices
4 glacé cherries
100 g (4 oz) butter
100 g (4 oz) caster sugar
2 eggs
175 g (6 oz) self-raising flour
a little milk, if needed

Preheat the oven to 180°C (350°F) mark 4. Grease an 18-cm (7-inch) round cake tin and line it with buttered greaseproof paper. Even if it is a non-stick tin, do line it.

Coat the base with honey. Arrange the pineapple slices, with the cherries in the holes, on the honey. Cream the butter and sugar together until pale and fluffy. Beat in the eggs. Sieve the flour and fold into the mixture. Add a little milk to make a dropping consistency. Spoon it into the tin, level the top and bake for about 40 minutes.

Turn out the pudding and remove the paper carefully. Serve with warmed honey and lightly whipped cream.

To test a baked sponge mixture, open the oven gently, press the top of the sponge lightly with the fingertips. If it feels springy to the touch and is just beginning to shrink away from the sides of the tin, it is done. Practice makes perfect with this test.

LEMON SURPRISE

Serves 4

50 g (2 oz) butter
100 g (4 oz) caster sugar
grated rind and juice of 1 lemon
2 eggs, separated
25 g (1 oz) plain flour
275 ml (½ pint) milk

Heat the oven to 180°C (350°F) mark 4. Butter a 1-litre (2-pint) pie dish. Cream the butter with the sugar until pale and fluffy. Beat the lemon rind into the butter and sugar. Beat in the egg yolks. Sieve the flour and add it by degrees with the milk followed by the lemon juice. (It will curdle now but do not worry.)

Beat the egg whites stiffly and fold evenly into the mixture. Turn into the pie dish and bake for about 40 minutes, until golden brown. You will find that the curdled mixture has separated into a lemon custard with a sponge top.

CHOCOLATE PUDDING

Serves 4–5

225 g (8 oz) self-raising flour
½ tsp salt
1 tbsp cocoa
100 g (4 oz) shredded suet
2 tbsp caster sugar
150 ml (¼ pint) milk

Grease a 750-ml (1½-pint) basin. Sift the flour, salt and cocoa into a bowl, add the suet and sugar and mix well together. Add the milk and mix to a soft dropping consistency.

Turn into a basin and cover with pleated greaseproof paper and a pudding cloth or foil. Steam for 2 hours. Turn out and serve with hazelnut yoghurt or with a hot chocolate sauce.

FUDGE PUDDING

Serves 4–5

4 slices bread (brown or white)
25 g (1 oz) raisins
25 g (1 oz) glacé cherries, quartered
25 g (1 oz) soft brown sugar
1 tbsp ground almonds
50 g (2 oz) granulated sugar
2 tbsp water
2 eggs
275 ml (½ pint) milk

Butter a 750-ml (1½-pint) pudding basin.
Cut the bread into cubes. Put into a bowl
and mix with the raisins, cherries, sugar and
ground almonds.

Gently heat the granulated sugar in the
water in a heavy-based pan until melted. Do
not stir. Turn up the heat and darken to a
honey brown. Take off the heat and cool.
Beat the eggs. Add the milk and the
caramel. Stir and pour the mixture around
and over the bread.

Leave to soak for 10 minutes. Turn into
the basin. Cover with pleated greaseproof
paper and a pudding cloth or foil and steam
for 1 hour. Turn out and serve.

RAISIN PUDDING

Serves 4

100 g (4 oz) stoned raisins
100 g (4 oz) butter
100 g (4 oz) caster sugar
2 eggs
100 g (4 oz) self-raising flour

Line a greased 750-ml (1½-pint) pudding
basin with the raisins (they *do* stick on).
Cream the butter and sugar until light and
fluffy. Beat the eggs. Sieve the flour and
fold into the mixture with alternate
spoonfuls of egg. Very gently spoon it into
the basin, which should be no more than
three-quarters full. All steamed puddings
should expand.

Cover as usual with pleated greaseproof
paper and a pudding cloth or foil. Steam for
1¾ hours.

Without the raisins this is a canary pudding,
or if cooked in individual moulds, it becomes
castle puddings, and of course if you change
your mind half way through, it is a Victoria
sandwich mixture.

POOR KNIGHTS OF WINDSOR

Allow 2 for each person

bread – a sliced loaf does well
150 ml (¼ pint) milk
50 g (2 oz) caster sugar
1 egg
butter and sunflower or corn oil

Cut the bread into 5-cm (2-inch) wide fingers. Warm the milk, sweeten it to taste. Beat the egg. Soak the fingers in the sweet milk. Drain. Dip in the beaten egg. Fry in sizzling butter and oil (the oil stops the butter burning). Serve piping hot with melted golden syrup or warmed jam.

Variation
The Swedish go one better with rich knights – *Rika Riddane*. Prepare as poor knights, but after the egg dip, draw the slices through chopped almonds and sugar before frying. Serve these rich fellows, of course, with cream.

SPICED LAYER PUDDING

Serves 4

225 g (8 oz) self-raising flour
½ tsp salt
50 g (2 oz) caster sugar
100 g (4 oz) shredded suet
150 ml (¼ pint) cold water
50 g (2 oz) margarine
100 g (4 oz) cut mixed peel
1 tsp ground cinnamon or mixed spice

Sieve the flour and salt together. Add the sugar and suet and mix well. Add the water to form a softish dough. Divide into four graduated pieces. Soften the margarine and blend it with the mixed peel.

Grease a 750-ml (1½-pint) pudding basin and roll out the smallest piece of dough to fit the base. Spread with the mixed peel and give a light sprinkling of spice. Roll out a slightly larger piece and proceed as before. Add the third round with the mixture spread on it and the spice. Use the last round for the top.

Cover with pleated greaseproof paper and a pudding cloth or foil. Steam for 2 hours. Turn out and serve with custard sauce.

PASTRY DESSERTS

Pastries are a natural base for puddings and desserts. So many flavours, fruits and creams can be used for fillings, and the finished dish can be quick and simple for every day, or dressed up to make an elegant dessert for a party.

Pastry making is an art, but one quickly and easily mastered. The secret is to have everything cool – both ingredients and utensils – and to use only the fingertips when rubbing in to keep the pastry light and airy. It is the air incorporated into the dough which gives the characteristic texture to each type of pastry. Different pastries are made with varying proportions of fat to flour, and it is the method of rolling and folding or rubbing in which defines the type of pastry.

Once made, pastry will freeze for up to 6 months if suitably wrapped in thick foil or polythene. This means it is possible to make up large quantities and freeze the surplus for future use.

Cornflour is good for dredging the pastry board. It is so light that it brushes off the pastry easily and does not unbalance the recipe.

The flans and tarts in this chapter are made and baked in various ways with a wide selection of fillings. Take care when making the pastry, for it is a very important part of the recipe.

To 'blake blind', heat the oven to 200°C (400°F) mark 6 for short crust pastry or 220°C (425°F) mark 7 for flaky pastry. Line the pastry case with greaseproof paper, non-stick paper or foil and fill it with baking beans. Cook for 15 minutes standing on a hot baking sheet. Remove the beans and paper or foil and return to the oven for a further 5–10 minutes to dry out. Let the pastry cool before either lifting off the flan ring or removing from a tin or plate.

For baking beans, use any dried bean such as haricot, or dried lentils or rice. Retain and store for continual use. Pseudo 'beans' made of synthetic material are also available in some shops.

As an alternative to a fluted china flan dish, heavy flan tins can be bought at good kitchen shops. Tin is a superb conductor of heat which means that the base of the flan is always cooked. Oblong tins are also available, about 28 x 20 cm (11 x 8 inch), or individual ones, all with loose bottoms. Lard them well and bake blind in a hot oven to prove them before use. Line the base with non-stick parchment.

PÂTE SUCRÉE

225 g (8 oz) plain flour
¼ tsp salt
150 g (5 oz) butter
25 g (1 oz) sieved icing sugar or
  caster sugar
2 egg yolks
a little cold water if needed

Sieve the flour and salt into a basin. Rub in the butter lightly and quickly. Sprinkle in the sugar. Beat the egg yolks. Make a well in the flour, add the egg yolks and mix well. Gradually draw down the flour from the sides and work it all in with the fingertips. It should be a firm yet soft dough, so add a teaspoon or two of cold water if necessary. Cover and leave to rest in a cool place for 20 minutes. Use as required.

Cook at 190°C (375°F) mark 5, or according to the recipe.

SHORT CRUST PASTRY

225 g (8 oz) plain flour
¼ tsp salt
50 g (2 oz) block margarine
50 g (2 oz) lard
about 3 tbsp cold water

Sieve the flour and salt into a bowl. Add the fats and rub quickly and lightly together with the fingertips until the mixture resembles fine breadcrumbs. Add the water a little at a time. Cut and stir with a knife until the mixture holds together. Turn on to a lightly floured board and knead lightly until the dough is smooth. Cover and chill until required.

FLAKY PASTRY

175 g (6 oz) plain flour
¼ tsp salt
50 g (2 oz) butter
50 g (2 oz) lard
3–4 tbsp cold water

Sieve the flour and salt into a bowl. Mix the butter and lard quickly together and divide into four. Chill. Rub one part of the fat into the flour then mix to a firm dough with the water. Knead lightly on a floured surface then roll out to a strip three times as long as it is wide. Dot the second portion of fat in small flakes on the lower two-thirds of the pastry.

Fold the bottom third of the pastry upwards and the top third downwards, seal the edges. Cover and chill for 15 minutes.

Remove the pastry from its wrapping and with the folded side to the right, roll out again to a strip three times as long as it is wide. Repeat the 'flaking' process with the third portion of fat, fold and chill as before.

Repeat the rolling, flaking and folding process again, chill, then repeat for a final time but without adding any fat. Wrap and chill for 15–30 minutes before use.

Cook at 220°C (425°F) mark 7, or follow the times suggested in the individual recipes which follow.

CRÈME CHANTILLY

1 egg white
275 ml (½ pint) double or whipping
  cream
2 tsp caster sugar

Stiffly whisk the egg white. Whip the cream
carefully with the sugar until very thick.
Fold the egg white gently but thoroughly
into the whipped cream.

Keep a vanilla pod in the jar of caster sugar
instead of using vanilla essence (and *never*
use vanilla flavouring). 'Whipping cream' is
now available everywhere. Its use does seem
to prevent the sudden and unwelcome
drama of butter-making which can so easily
overtake the unwary when whipping double
cream.

APRICOT GLAZE

6 tbsp apricot jam
75 ml (3 fl oz) water
1 tsp lemon juice

Put the jam and water into a pan and
simmer for a few minutes, stirring well.
Bring to the boil and cook for 3 minutes
longer. Stir in the lemon juice. The glaze
should just drop from the spoon. For a
smooth glaze, sieve or blend to remove any
lumps of fruit.

TREACLE TART

Serves 6

225 g (8 oz) short crust pastry (see
  page 17)
175 g (6 oz) golden syrup
50 g (2 oz) fresh white breadcrumbs
1 tsp lemon juice

Heat the oven to 190°C (375°F) mark 5.
Make the pastry. Cut off a quarter to lattice
the top. Roll out the remainder and use to
line a buttered 20-cm (8-inch) ovenproof
plate. Flute the edges.

Warm the syrup in a saucepan, add the
breadcrumbs and lemon juice and pour on
to the pastry. Roll out the remaining pastry
and cut it into narrow strips to twist.
Criss-cross the strips over the treacle,
sticking the ends on to the edges of the tart
with water. Bake for 30 minutes. Serve hot
or cold.

APPLE CHAUSSON

Serves 6

175 g (6 oz) flaky pastry (see
  page 17)
450 g (1 lb) cooking apples
50 g (2 oz) butter
75 g (3 oz) currants and sultanas
  mixed
grated rind of 1 lemon
brown sugar
caster sugar

Heat the oven to 200°C (400°F) mark 6.
Make the pastry and leave it to relax for
about 20 minutes in the refrigerator. Peel,
core and thickly slice the apples. Melt the
butter in a pan. Add the apples in layers
with the dried fruit (check for stalks),
lemon rind, and brown sugar to taste. Keep
on a low heat for 5–10 minutes, shaking the
pan from time to time. Turn out to cool.
The apples will be buttery but not cooked.

Divide the pastry in half and roll out into
two 20-cm (8-inch) circles. Put one circle on
to a baking sheet and spoon on the apples,
leaving a 2.5-cm (1-inch) margin of pastry
round the edge; brush the margin with
water. Put the remaining circle of pastry on
top and press the edges together. Trim.
Make the classic pattern on the top with the
point of a knife – six or eight curved lines
from the middle to the edge, and two circles
around the edge. Brush with water, sprinkle
with caster sugar and cook for 40 minutes.

PINEAPPLE CURD TART

Serves 4–6

175 g (6 oz) short crust pastry (see page 17)
225 g (8 oz) cream cheese
2 tbsp granulated sugar
2 egg yolks
150 ml (¼ pint) single cream
425-g (15-oz) can pineapple rings

Heat the oven to 180°C (350°F) mark 4. Roll out the pastry to 5 mm (¼ inch) thick and use to line a 20-cm (8-inch) fluted ovenproof flan case (or use a flan ring). Press the pastry down well and prick the base.

Beat the cheese until smooth, add the sugar, egg yolks and cream. Turn the mixture into the pastry case and bake until it is firm to the fingertips, about 20–30 minutes.

In the meantime, poach the pineapple slices in their own syrup until almost caramelised. This needs care. When the cake is cooked, leave until cold. Arrange the pineapple slices on the top and spoon any remaining syrup on to them.

FRESH RASPBERRY TARTLETS

Makes 16–20

225 g (8 oz) shortcrust pastry (see page 17)
450 g (1 lb) raspberries
225 g (8 oz) raspberry jam
1 tbsp water

Heat the oven to 190°C (375°F) mark 5. Make the pastry and roll out to 5 mm (¼ inch) thick. Cut 16–20 rounds using a fluted cutter. Turn the rounds over and use to line patty tins. Bake blind (see page 15) for 15 minutes. Remove the paper and beans and return to the oven for a further 10 minutes. Cool on a wire rack.

Hull and pick over the fruit. Arrange in the tartlets, pointed end uppermost. Put the jam in a saucepan, add the water. Bring to the boil, stirring all the time, then cool. Run through a sieve or the fine plate of a mouli-legume. Carefully spoon the warm jam over the tartlets. Hand round whipped cream separately.

These empty tartlets freeze perfectly, as does all flour confectionery.

CUSTARD TART

Serves 4–6

175 g (6 oz) pâte sucrée (see
  page 16)
275 ml (½ pint) milk
1 egg
2 egg yolks
15 g (½ oz) caster sugar
a scrape of nutmeg

Heat the oven to 200°C (400°F) mark 6. Butter a 20-cm (8-inch) ovenproof fluted china flan case. Roll out the pastry as thinly as possible on a board lightly dusted with cornflour. Lift on to the rolling pin (flan pastry is more difficult to handle than ordinary short crust) and use to line the flan case. Using a little ball of pastry as a pusher, press out all the air which is trapped between the pastry and the case. Prick the pastry and press again. Cook on a baking sheet for about 15 minutes. Meanwhile make the custard.

Boil the milk. Beat the egg and the yolks with the sugar. Pour the boiling milk over them, beating all the time. Beat for another few minutes, by which time the flan case should be cooked. Pull the oven rack with the flan case a little way out of the oven, and with a jug, gently pour the custard into the case. Sprinkle with a little grated nutmeg. Ease gently back into the oven and cook for about 30 minutes until set.

Egg yolks make a custard creamy and egg whites set it, which is why the recipes use the rather irritating proportion of yolks to whole eggs. It is worth doing just what is suggested for a creamy, well set custard. If whole eggs are used, the custard will be too firm.

BLACKCURRANT TART

Serves 4

175 g (6 oz) pâte sucrée (see
page 16)
225 g (8 oz) prepared blackcurrants
100 g (4 oz) caster sugar
1 tsp ground cinnamon
caster sugar for dredging

Heat the oven to 200°C (400°F) mark 6.
Roll out the pastry and use to line an
18-cm (7-inch) fluted china flan dish
Reserve the trimmings.

Simmer the blackcurrants in their own
juice with the sugar and cinnamon, stirring
all the time until the mixture is thick and
glossy. This is called a 'marmelade'. Cool a
little and turn into the flan case. Roll out the
pastry trimmings, cut into narrow strips
and make a twisted lattice top for the tart.
Brush with water and sprinkle with caster
sugar to glaze.

Bake in the centre of the oven on a hot
baking sheet for 30–35 minutes.

ORANGE AND APPLE FLAN

Serves 4

175 g (6 oz) pâte sucrée (see
page 16)
700 g (1½ lb) cooking apples
2 oranges
50 g (2 oz) granulated sugar
caster sugar
apricot glaze (see page 18)

Heat the oven to 200°C (400°F) mark 6. Roll
out the pastry and use to line an 18-cm
(7-inch) fluted china flan dish. Push well
into the base with a little ball of pastry.

Peel, core and slice the apples. Grate the
rind and squeeze the juice of one orange.
Put the apples with the sugar and the orange
rind and juice into a pan and simmer until
reduced to a thick pulp. Depending on the
apples, you may need a tablespoon of water
to prevent the fruit from catching. Fill the
flan with the apple. Stand the flan on a
baking sheet and dust with caster sugar.
Bake in the centre of the oven for
30 minutes.

With a sharp knife, cut away the peel and
all the pith from the other orange. Slice very
thinly and when the flan is cooked, put
overlapping circles of orange on the apple.
Brush with apricot glaze. Serve warm.

FRESH STRAWBERRY FLAN

Serves 6

1 packet strawberry jelly
225 g (8 oz) pâte sucrée (see
   page 16)
450 g (1 lb) strawberries
150 ml (¼ pint) double cream

Make the jelly and leave it to cool almost to setting point. Heat the oven to 190°C (375°F) mark 5. Make the pastry and use it to line a 20-cm (8-inch) ovenproof fluted china flan dish. Bake blind for 20 minutes (see page 15). Cool. If you are turning it out, *now* is the moment for that.

Arrange the hulled strawberries in the flan case, pointed ends upwards. Spoon just enough of the setting (but not set) jelly over the strawberries to barely cover them. Leave the remaining jelly to set then chop it and use to decorate around the top edge of the flan. Whip the cream and pile very neatly into the centre of the flan.

CHESTNUT TORTE

Serves 4–6

225 g (8 oz) pâte sucrée (see
   page 16)
225-g (8-oz) can chestnut purée
275 ml (½ pint) crème chantilly (see
   page 18)
50 g (2 oz) plain chocolate, grated
icing sugar

Heat the oven to 190°C (375°F) mark 5. Make the pastry and divide into three portions. Roll each piece as thinly as possible into an 20-cm (8-inch) circle. Trim using a plate and a sharp knife. Cook on a baking sheet for 20 minutes. Cool on a wire rack.

Break up the chestnut purée with a fork, and very gently fold the crème chantilly into it. Spread the filling generously on two of the pastry circles and sandwich together. Carefully cut the third circle into six segments, pressing down with a sharp knife. Arrange the six segments on top of the crème chantilly. Cover with grated chocolate and dust with icing sugar.

CUSTARDS, CREAMS AND JELLIES

Here is a selection of simple but delicious
recipes fit to grace any table. Old favourites
such as trifle and crème brulée appear alongside
jellies and custard-based recipes, together with
plenty of new and interesting ideas.

Custards and creams should be smooth and creamy and jellies well set but by no means firm, for flavour is linked to texture in these delicate dishes. Although ideal milk is fine for the family there is absolutely nothing like cream and it is not really very extravagant. If you need to cook for more people than the recipe says, make two layers instead of one, and perhaps use a different flavour or colour.

CRÈME À LA VANILLE

575 ml (1 pint) milk
25 g (1 oz) caster sugar
1 vanilla pod
4 egg yolks

Heat the milk to just below boiling with the sugar and the vanilla pod. Beat the egg yolks. Discard the vanilla pod and then pour the milk slowly on to the egg yolks, beating all the time. Return to a gentle heat and, stirring continuously, cook until the custard coats the back of a spoon. Turn into a bowl and cool, with a piece of damp greaseproof paper touching the surface of the custard to prevent a skin forming.

This is known as a 'boiled' custard, which it most certainly must not be, or it will curdle. It is the basic egg custard used for many of these recipes. The addition of a teaspoon of cornflour or custard powder at the mixing stage will help the inexperienced cook to prevent any risk of curdling the custard.

It is worth persevering with the genuine article, for it is beyond compare when properly made, and the basis for many superb desserts.

OLD ENGLISH TRIFLE

Serves 4

175 g (6 oz) sponge cake
75 ml (3 fl oz) dry sherry
3 tbsp raspberry jam
3 egg yolks
1 tsp caster sugar
1 vanilla pod
425 ml (¾ pint) milk
150 ml (¼ pint) double cream
angelica, almonds, ratafia biscuits,
  glacé cherries

Put the sponge cake in a glass dish. Soak with sherry and dot with the raspberry jam. Use the egg yolks, sugar, vanilla pod and milk to make a crème à la vanille (see page 25). Pour over the sponge cake and leave until set.

Whip the cream and spoon on to the custard. Decorate with small diamonds of angelica, blanched split almonds, ratafia biscuits and a few cherries.

This is a classic trifle which has no jelly and no fruit. It is easy to make, but take care not to let the custard curdle.

CRÈME BAVAROISE

Serves 4

2 eggs, separated
50 g (2 oz) caster sugar
275 ml (½ pint) milk
1 vanilla pod
15 g (½ oz) powdered gelatine
150 ml (¼ pint) double or whipping
  cream

Whisk the egg yolks with the sugar until pale. Heat the milk with the vanilla pod. Leave to infuse while you dissolve the gelatine in a bowl with 2 tablespoons water, standing in a pan of hot water. Remove the vanilla pod. Pour the hot milk on to the yolks, beating all the time. Cook slowly over hot water until the yolks begin to thicken, beating all the time. Add the gelatine to this mixture, pouring it in a thin stream as you stir. Let the mixture cool.

Whisk the egg whites stiffly and whip the cream. Fold the cream and egg whites together. Stir a little into the custard (this helps to give an even texture) then fold in the remainder, thoroughly but carefully.

Spoon into individual glasses, and leave to set.

The crème may be flavoured with chocolate, coffee or fruit.

CRÈME BRULÉE

Serves 4
4 egg yolks
25 g (1 oz) caster sugar
1 vanilla pod
575 ml (1 pint) double cream
extra caster sugar

Beat the egg yolks with the sugar until light and fluffy. Put the vanilla pod into the cream in the top of a double saucepan, or a basin over a saucepan of hot water. Bring the cream *almost* to the boil (but it must *not* boil). Remove the vanilla pod.

Pour the cream on to the egg yolks, stirring all the time. Return to the double saucepan and cook gently until it thickens, stirring all the time. Pour into a shallow dish and leave to stand for several hours and chill.

Before serving, dust with an even layer of caster sugar and brown carefully under a moderate grill. Serve at once.

This rich dessert is a speciality of Trinity College, Cambridge.

BANANA CUSTARD

Serves 4–6

575 ml (1 pint) crème à la vanille
  made with brown sugar (see
  page 25)
75 g (3 oz) soft brown sugar
75 g (3 oz) butter
3 bananas

Make up the custard as usual, but using brown sugar instead of caster. Melt the sugar and the butter in a frying pan. Peel and slice the bananas. Gently poach them in the sugar until soft.

Put a layer of bananas in the bottom of a glass bowl and cover with custard. Continue to layer until the fruit is used up. Finish with a layer of custard.

A round of damp greaseproof paper pressed lightly on the top of the custard prevents a skin from forming, or alternatively, cover the dish with cling film.

ORANGE JELLY

Serves 4

75 g (3 oz) lump sugar
3 oranges
1 lemon
15 g (½ oz) powdered gelatine
275 ml (½ pint) cold water or fresh
    or canned orange juice

Rub the sugar lumps over the rinds of the fruit. Squeeze the juice. Dissolve the gelatine in 2 tablespoons water over a pan of hot water. Add to the fruit juices in a pan, with the sugar. Make up to 425 ml (¾ pint) with water, or with fresh or canned orange juice. Heat the mixture gently to melt the sugar, then pour into a wetted mould and leave to set. Chill thoroughly before turning out. Serve with whipped cream.

CHRISTMAS JELLY

Serves 4

275 ml (½ pint) water
two 10-cm (4-inch) cinnamon sticks
4 cloves
4 blades mace
1 packet blackcurrant jelly
150 ml (¼ pint) port

Simmer the spices in the water for 10 minutes. Stand for 1 hour. Strain and warm again. Melt the jelly in the spicy water. Add the port and make up to 575 ml (1 pint) with cold water. Transfer to a jelly mould or into individual glasses and chill until set.

Best served in tall, sparkling, individual glasses. Its lovely rich colour and warm taste need no further adornment.

APPLE JELLY

Serves 4–6

450 g (1 lb) cooking apples
2 cloves
25 g (1 oz) caster sugar
1 lemon
2 tbsp bramble jelly
15 g (½ oz) powdered gelatine

Peel, core and slice the apples. Cook with the cloves and sugar in very little water (Bramleys will need none). Discard the cloves and beat the apples to a cream. Grate the rind and squeeze the juice from the lemon; stir into the apples with the bramble jelly.

    Dissolve the gelatine in 2 tablespoons water in a bowl over a pan of hot water.

Fold evenly into the apples, stirring all the time. Turn into a wet mould and leave to set. Turn out and serve with cream and homemade almond tuilles or other decorative biscuits.

This is a particularly easy and delicious pudding.

CRÈME CARAMEL

Serves 4

75 g (3 oz) caster sugar
4 eggs
4 egg yolks
2 tbsp sugar
575 ml (1 pint) milk
1 vanilla pod

Heat the oven to 180°C (350°F) mark 4. Put the sugar with 1 teaspoon water in a heavy-based saucepan and melt slowly without stirring. When it starts colouring, stir equally slowly and carefully until it is a dark honey colour. Pour this caramel into a warm china soufflé dish. Turn it round and about to coat the sides and base.

Break the eggs into a bowl, add the yolks and sugar and beat well. Boil the milk with the vanilla pod. Remove the pod and pour the milk on to the eggs, beating all the time. Pour carefully into the caramel-lined dish. Stand in a roasting tin containing 4 cm (1½ inches) water and cook until the custard is set – about 40 minutes. Remove from the oven and leave until cold, then chill before turning out.

This, as with all baked custards, does very well in a slow cooker.

PINEAPPLE CHARLOTTE

Serves 4–6

575 ml (1 pint) milk
4 egg yolks
1 tsp arrowroot or cornflour
50 g (2 oz) caster sugar
425-g (15-oz) can pineapple rings
275 ml (½ pint) double or whipping
  cream
15 g (½ oz) powdered gelatine
2 eggs whites
1 packet sponge fingers

Heat the milk. Beat the egg yolks with the arrowroot and sugar. Pour the hot milk on to the eggs, beating all the time, then leave to cool. Drain the pineapple. Keep the juice. Cut up half the rings to give about 4 tablespoons. Whip the cream fairly lightly.

Soak the gelatine in 3–4 tablespoons of pineapple juice (it is *fresh* pineapple that stops gelatine setting). Dissolve over a pan of hot water. Pour into the custard in a thin stream, then fold in three-quarters of the cream. Leave until the custard starts to set, then whisk the egg whites stiffly and fold them, with the chopped pineapple into the charlotte, with a metal spoon. Turn into a greased charlotte mould, a china soufflé dish or a cake tin. Chill until set.

Turn out carefully on to a serving dish. Spread the sides with the rest of the cream and stick the sponge fingers around the sides. Decorate the top with the remaining pineapple rings.

Spring release cake tins make this recipe much easier, and are worthwhile investing in if you do much entertaining.

ICE COLD ZABAGLIONE

Serves 4

50 g (2 oz) sugar
1 tbsp water
1 egg
2 egg yolks
1 tbsp Marsala

Melt the sugar with the water in a strong saucepan. Bring to the boil until bubbling and syrupy. Take off the heat. Separate the egg. Beat the egg white until stiff. Pour the syrup on to it and beat until it is absorbed. This makes a meringue mixture.

Put the 3 egg yolks with the Marsala into

a bowl. Whisk over a saucepan of hot water until thick, then fold into the meringue mixture. Pour into glasses and refrigerate until ice cold. Serve with sponge fingers and cream.

This can be served warm: it is made by beating 3 egg yolks with the sugar and Marsala over heat until thick. It is easier to make, but must be served at once, which could be a bore if you are cooking for a dinner party.

GOOSEBERRY WHIP

Serves 4–6

450 g (1 lb) gooseberries
100 ml (4 fl oz) white wine
100 ml (4 fl oz) water
thinly pared rind of 1 lemon
100 g (4 oz) sugar
2 eggs
walnut halves or almonds to decorate

Top and tail the gooseberries and wash them. Simmer until tender with the wine, water and lemon rind. Sieve to remove the seeds. Return to the pan and cook over a gentle heat. Add the sugar and stir until dissolved. Remove from the heat and cool.
　　Separate the eggs. Beat the yolks and fold into the mixture. Whisk the egg whites stiffly and fold into the gooseberry mixture.
　　Pour into individual glasses and decorate with a walnut or a blanched almond.

FRUIT FOR ALL SEASONS

The mouth-watering recipes in this chapter range from light summer dishes made with fresh fruit to substantial cooked puddings. A few delicious time-saving recipes using canned fruits have also been included.

'Stewing' fruit in water and sugar can all too often result in a sort of 'wash-day afters'. If the trouble is taken to make a syrup first, then adding the prepared fruit, poaching it and simmering carefully until the fruit is cooked, all the richness and texture of the fruit is retained. A cheap frying pan kept only for fruit and meringue poaching is a very handy item of equipment.

Canned fruit can often be substituted for fresh fruit, though it may need a little extra attention. Poaching canned peaches or pears in their own syrup, for example, improves the texture and flavour beyond belief.

LIGHT SUGAR SYRUP

100 g (4 oz) granulated sugar
225–275 ml (8–10 fl oz) water

Dissolve every grain of sugar in the water before bringing it to the boil, then boil for 2 minutes. This syrup keeps well. If the fruit is very sour, do not make the syrup heavier, but simply add a little extra sugar while the fruit is still hot.

If you keep a vanilla pod in your sugar jar, this greatly improves the flavour of the fruit, as well as many other dishes.

JAMAICAN BANANAS

Serves 4–6

6 bananas
2 tbsp rum
4 tsp soft brown sugar
25 g (1 oz) flaked almonds
225 ml (8 fl oz) evaporated milk,
   chilled
4 tsp instant coffee powder

Slice the bananas into a glass bowl. Cover them with the rum and brown sugar. Toast the almonds under the grill or in a pan. They burn easily so watch carefully.

Chill the evaporated milk for 24 hours, then it will whip quite easily. Whip the evaporated milk, adding the coffee little by little. Cover the bananas with the coffee cream and sprinkle with toasted almonds.

When cooking with instant coffee, always use a good quality one.

PINEAPPLE FLAMBÉ

Serves 4–6

440-g (15½-oz) can pineapple rings
   or a fresh pineapple
caster sugar
50 g (2 oz) butter
50 ml (2 fl oz) brandy or rum

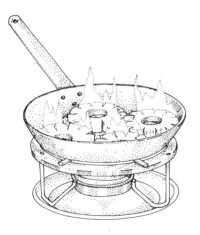

Strain the pineapple rings. There will be six or seven. Keep the juice for something else. If a fresh pineapple is used, peel, core and slice it. Dust the rings with caster sugar.

Sizzle the butter in a frying pan. Put in as many rings as you can and brown them. The sugar will caramelise. Take out one or two to make room for the spares. Brown them too. Return them all to the pan, sprinkle again with sugar and get them really hot.

Pour the brandy or rum over the pineapple rings. It will probably light at once. If not, set a match to it. Serve while flaming.

If you have a suitable frying pan you can prepare half of this in the kitchen and then put it over a burner in the dining room. The little methylated spirit lamp under a fondue dish is first class for this – but a chafing dish is the proper job.

Bananas are equally delicious for this.

GOLDEN CHARTREUSE

Serves 4–6

*300-g (11-oz) can Cape
 goldenberries*
300-g (11-oz) can mandarin oranges
425-g (15-oz) can peaches
1 packet lemon jelly
1 packet orange jelly

Drain the fruit as the juices will be too sweet to use. Make up the jellies together following instructions on the packet. Cool almost to setting point.

Using a 1½-litre (2½-pint) glass dish or jelly mould, put some jelly in the bottom, then a layer of goldenberries. Add a layer of jelly and chill until set. Cover with a layer of mandarins, pour jelly over them and leave to set. Then arrange a layer of thinly sliced peaches over the set jelly; cover with more jelly and leave to set. Continue until all the fruit and jelly is used up. Leave to set firmly in the refrigerator.

To turn out, dip the mould briefly in hot water and invert on to a serving dish. If serving in the dish, a chiffonade of chopped jelly on the top is attractive.

For a buffet luncheon, melt the jellies separately and make up as above but in glasses, using the jellies alternately.

RHUBARB FOOL

Serves 4

450 g (1 lb) rhubarb
*150 ml (¼ pint) sugar syrup (see
 page 33)*
2 tsp custard powder
150 ml (¼ pint) milk
sugar
*150 ml (¼ pint) double or whipping
 cream*

Prepare the rhubarb, trim and cut it into short lengths. Poach in the sugar syrup until tender. Strain the rhubarb and leave to cool. Make the custard with the milk according to instructions on the packet. Sweeten to taste and cool. If the rhubarb is very soft, mix it up with a wooden fork. If not, rub it through a sieve, then sweeten to taste.

Fold the custard into the rhubarb. Whip the cream and fold through the mixture very lightly so that it all looks streaky.

Chill thoroughly and serve in glasses with sponge fingers.

MELON SURPRISE

Serves 4–6

1 honeydew melon
225 g (8 oz) fresh strawberries or
   raspberries
1 fresh peach, peeled and stoned
1 dessert pear, peeled and cored
75 g (3 oz) caster sugar
2 tbsp dry sherry

Cut the top off the melon and reserve as a lid. Cut a very small slice off the base of the melon so that it will stand. Scoop out the seeds. Take out the flesh in balls with a vegetable scoop or a strong teaspoon. Be careful not to go through the side. Put the melon balls in a bowl, and the melon shell and lid in a polythene bag, and put them all in the refrigerator to chill. (The bag is a must because otherwise the smell of melon will filter into everything else in the refrigerator.)

Pick over and hull the strawberries or raspberries. Reserve a few and add the rest to the melon balls. Dice the peach and pear and add to the fruit in the bowl. Sprinkle the fruit with caster sugar and sherry and leave to stand for half an hour.

Take out the melon shell and fill it carefully with fruit mixture, finishing with the melon balls. Add the reserved strawberries or raspberries and put the melon lid on top. To serve, sit the melon on two or three vine leaves, if available, on an attractive plate.

PLUM COMPÔTE

Serves 4

450 g (1 lb) plums
1 glass port
50 g (2 oz) redcurrant jelly
grated rind and juice of 1 orange
approx. 50 g (2 oz) sugar

Wipe the plums, halve and remove the stones. Put the port, jelly, the grated rind and juice of the orange and the sugar into a frying pan. Heat gently to melt the jelly and sugar. Add the plums to this syrup, cut sides down, and poach – for that is what it is – for 10–15 minutes, spooning the syrup over the plums. Cool a little, then spoon carefully into a bowl. Pour the remaining syrup over the plums.

Serve with thin slices of sponge cake or sponge fingers.

APPLE FLORENTINE

Serves 4–6

700 g (1½ lb) cooking apples
50 g (2 oz) butter
2 tsp cooking oil
75 g (3 oz) soft brown sugar
¼ tsp ground cinnamon
grated rind of 2 lemons
225 g (8 oz) flaky pastry (see
    page 17)
a little milk
150 ml (¼ pint) cider
nutmeg
5-cm (2-inch) cinnamon stick
icing sugar

Heat the oven to 220°C (425°F) mark 7. Peel and core the apples and cut into quarters but no smaller. Fry in the butter and oil until beginning to colour. Sprinkle with the sugar, cinnamon and grated rind of one lemon. Turn into a round ovenproof dish or shallow pie dish. Dampen the edge.

Roll out the pastry 5 mm (¼ inch) thick and use it to cover the apples. Press the pastry down on the edge and trim. Glaze lightly with milk and cook for 30 minutes. Spice the cider by heating it in a small saucepan with a good grating of nutmeg, the cinnamon stick and the grated rind of the second lemon. Let it stand for 20 minutes, add sugar to taste, and then strain.

When the pastry is done, lift it off the pie by running a knife between the edge and the dish. Cut it into segments. Pour the hot spiced cider into the dish. Put the pastry pieces back in place and dust with icing sugar. Serve with thick cream.

APPLE SNOW

Serves 4–6

grated rind and juice of 1 lemon
575 ml (1 pint) apple purée
50 g (2 oz) caster sugar
15 g (½ oz) powdered gelatine
2 tbsp water
2 egg whites

Add the lemon rind and juice to the apple purée with the sugar. Dissolve the gelatine in the water in a bowl over a pan of hot water. Pour in a thin stream into the purée, beating all the time.

Whisk the egg whites stiffly. Fold into the purée with a metal spoon. Serve in individual glasses with sponge fingers.

Traditionally 'snows' are not set with gelatine and must be served soon after they are made. This one, however, can be made the day before.

BAKED APPLES

Serves 4

4 large cooking apples
2 tbsp raisins
1 tbsp mixed peel
golden syrup

Heat the oven to 180°C (350°F) mark 4. Peel the apples and remove the cores with a corer or potato peeler. Put them in a buttered pie dish. Fill the cavities with the raisins and mixed peel or any other kind of filling if preferred.

Pour melted golden syrup over the apples and cover the dish with a lid or foil. Bake until tender – 45–60 minutes.

LIMOGES CLAFOUTIS

Serves 4–6

700 g (1½ lb) fresh, ripe, cherries
3 eggs
50 g (2 oz) plain flour
¼ tsp salt
50 g (2 oz) caster sugar
425 ml (¾ pint) milk
50 g (2 oz) butter

Heat the oven to 220°C (425°F) mark 7. Stone the cherries. Beat the eggs, flour, salt and sugar together. Warm the milk and pour on to the egg mixture, beating all the time. Leave to stand for 20 minutes.

Butter a pie dish and put the cherries into it. Pour the egg mixture, which is a batter, over the cherries. Cook for 25–30 minutes.

APPLE AND BLACKBERRY CRUMBLE

Serves 4–6

4 cooking apples
450 g (1 lb) blackberries
2 tbsp sugar
50 g (2 oz) bramble jelly
150 g (5 oz) wholemeal flour
50 g (2 oz) demerara sugar
75 g (3 oz) butter
25 g (1 oz) chopped almonds

Heat the oven to 220°C (425°F) mark 7. Prepare and slice the apples. Wash and dry the blackberries. Put half the apples in the base of a buttered pie dish. Add all the blackberries with the sugar and bramble jelly. Cover with the remaining apples.

Mix the flour and sugar together and rub in the butter. Add the almonds and mix until they are thoroughly blended. Spread evenly over the fruit and cook for 20–30 minutes.

RANCIN

Serves 4–6

6 slices white bread
75 g (3 oz) butter
450 g (1 lb) black cherries
75 g (3 oz) caster sugar

Heat the oven to 200°C (400°F) mark 6. Spread the bread generously with butter – homemade bread is best, and homemade brioche is superb. Stone the cherries – use a cherry pitter or hook them out with a large hairpin. Put a layer of bread and butter, butter side up, in the base of an ovenproof dish.

Gently poach the cherries in as little water as possible with plenty of sugar. Spoon the cherries on to the bread, adding not too much juice. Cover with buttered bread, butter side up, and dust with sugar. Bake until brown and crisp – about 25 minutes.

This is a regional dish from Alsace.

RICE CONDÉ

65 g (2½ oz) Carolina rice
575 ml (1 pint) milk
1 vanilla pod
50 g (2 oz) caster sugar
15 g (½ oz) powdered gelatine
2 tbsp top of the milk

Cook the rice slowly in the milk with the vanilla pod and sugar for about 40 minutes. Cool. Remove the vanilla pod (wash it, dry it and put back in the sugar jar).

Dissolve the gelatine in 2 tablespoons water in a bowl over a pan of hot water. Fold through the rice with the top of the milk. Set in an appropriate mould.

PEAR CONDÉ

Serves 4–6

4 large pears
150 ml (¼ pint) sugar syrup (see page 33)
rice condé (see above)
glacé cherries
apricot glaze (see page 18)

Peel, halve and core the pears. Poach in sugar syrup until tender. If using canned pears, poach them in their own syrup. Leave in the syrup to cool. Drain the fruit and arrange on a bed of rice condé. Decorate sparingly with glacé cherries and coat with apricot glaze.

Almost any fruit is suitable for a condé.

PEASANT GIRL IN A VEIL

Serves 4–6

900 g (2 lb) ripe Victoria plums
100 g (4 oz) granulated sugar
175 g (6 oz) fresh white breadcrumbs
175 g (6 oz) butter
approx. 25 g (1 oz) caster sugar
150 ml (¼ pint) whipping cream
1 egg white

Heat the oven to 180°C (350°F) mark 4. Wipe the plums, slit the sides and take out the stones. Fill each cavity with a teaspoon of granulated sugar and a tiny knob of butter. Arrange the fruit, cut side up, in an ovenproof dish. Cover with caster sugar according to taste and cook for 30 minutes. Leave to cool.

Fry the crumbs lightly in 100 g (4 oz) butter and sprinkle over the plums. Whisk the egg white until stiff and lightly whisk the cream. Fold the two together and spoon over the plums.

SWEDISH RASPBERRY SHORTCAKE

Serves 6–8

100 g (4 oz) plain flour
75 g (3 oz) butter
25 g (1 oz) icing sugar
1 egg yolk
450 g (1 lb) raspberries
100 g (4 oz) redcurrant jelly
150 ml (¼ pint) whipping cream

Heat the oven to 190°C (375°F) mark 5. Sieve the flour into a bowl. Make a dip in it and put in the butter, sugar and egg yolk. Work with the fingertips, drawing the flour down from the sides until you have a smooth mixture. Cover and chill.

Use non-stick baking paper to line a baking sheet. Put the mixture on to it and pat it out into a round, about 5 mm (¼ inch) thick. Cover with greaseproof paper and beans and bake blind for 20 minutes (see page 15). Remove paper and beans and leave to cool. When cold arrange the raspberries, pointed end uppermost, over the pastry. Melt the redcurrant jelly (homemade is best) and spoon carefully over the raspberries.

Whip the cream and serve separately.

APRICOT AND WALNUT GALETTE

Serves 4–6

100 g (4 oz) walnut pieces
150 g (5 oz) plain flour
½ tsp salt
100 g (4 oz) butter
25 g (2 oz) caster sugar
icing sugar
225 g (8 oz) fresh or canned apricots
150 ml (¼ pint) whipping cream

Heat the oven to 180°C (350°F) mark 4. Run a rolling pin over the walnut pieces. Sieve the flour with the salt into a bowl. Sprinkle in the nuts. Make a dip in the flour and put the butter and sugar into it. Lightly draw the flour down from the sides and work until you have a smooth dough. The nuts will be incorporated as you work. Chill for 30 minutes.

Divide the dough into three pieces. Roll each into a circle about 15 cm (6 inches). Slip on to baking sheets lined with baking paper. Cook for 20–30 minutes. Cool.

Cut the apricots into quarters. Whip the cream and fold the fruit through it. When the pastry is cold sandwich together with the fruit and cream. Dust with icing sugar.

BLACKBERRY BETTY

Serves 4–6

4 cooking apples
175 g (6 oz) blackberries
50 g (2 oz) sugar
100 g (4 oz) fresh white
  breadcrumbs
50 g (2 oz) light soft brown sugar
50 g (2 oz) butter, melted

Peel, core and slice the apples. Poach them in very little water with the blackberries and sugar until tender. Cool.

Using individual glasses, layer the fruit, breadcrumbs, a little brown sugar and a spoonful of melted butter, continuing until you have used all the fruit. Finish with a layer of crumbs, sugar and butter. Top with a spoonful of cream if liked.

BAKED QUINCES

Serves 6

6 quinces
50 ml (2 fl oz) water
4 cloves
6 tbsp honey

Heat the oven to 150°C (300°F) mark 2. Peel the fruit and leave whole, with the stalks on if you can manage it. Stand the fruit, stalk end upwards, in an ovenproof dish with a good lid, with the water and the cloves. Spoon the honey over each quince. Cover tightly and cook for 2, or even 3, hours until tender. Serve chilled with whipped cream. This fruit turns the most ravishing colour and keeps its unique fragrance.

AUTUMN CREAM

Serves 6

450 g (1 lb) blackberries
5 tbsp blackcurrant syrup
1 tbsp brandy
175 g (6 oz) caster sugar
200 ml (8 fl oz) whipping cream
2 tbsp red wine
2 tbsp icing sugar, sieved

Pick the blackberries over. Put them in a bowl with the blackcurrant syrup (the sort you use for small children) and add the brandy. Sprinkle this with all the sugar and leave for several hours in the refrigerator.

When ready, spoon it carefully into tall individual glasses, leaving room for the cream. Whip the cream thickly, blending in the wine and icing sugar by degrees. The cream will turn pink and looks lovely on top of the blackberries.

HUNGARIAN PEACHES

Serves 4

4 large peaches
50 g (2 oz) ground almonds
50 g (2 oz) icing sugar, sieved
2 small bought sponge cakes
½ glass red wine
caster sugar

Heat the oven to 180°C (350°F) mark 4. Skin the peaches (pour boiling water over them then the skins come off easily). Halve, and remove the stone. Remove a little of the flesh to make a larger hole.

Mix the ground almonds and icing sugar with the sponge cakes and the spare peach flesh. Moisten with a little wine and use to stuff each peach half. Put the halves together, one on top of the other, and put in an ovenproof dish. Pour the rest of the wine over them and dust with caster sugar. Cook until the sugar caramelises; serve hot.

DAMSON SUÉDOISE

Serves 4–6

450 g (1 lb) damsons
175 g (6 oz) caster sugar
150 ml (¼ pint) water
15 g (½ oz) powdered gelatine

Stone the damsons. Put them with the sugar and water into a pan. Simmer slowly until the sugar is dissolved and the fruit tender. Blend the fruit or rub through a sieve. Make up to 575 ml (1 pint) with water.

Dissolve the gelatine in 2 tablespoons water in a bowl over a pan of hot water, and pour into the purée in a thin stream (this prevents the gelatine from 'stringing'). Mix well and pour the purée into a glass dish or mould. Set for several hours in the refrigerator.

Custard made from a packet, not too thickly, is surprisingly good with this.

A suédoise is a fruit purée set with gelatine.

PANCAKES, FRITTERS AND CHOUX

Pancakes are delicious and are now eaten all
year round, and not just on Shrove Tuesday,
when all the rich ingredients would be used up
in preparation for Lent. Nowadays there are as
many savoury fillings as sweet, but it takes a
lot to beat the traditional lemon
and sugar pancakes.

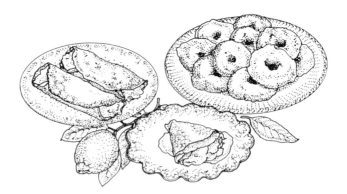

The basic pancake batter can be thinned down to make crêpes, those wonderful French delicacies which are really very simple to make at home. Pancake batter can be made using milk or a combination of milk and water. For really rich, thin pancakes, add an extra beaten egg.

Batter goes one further when used to coat fruits and then deep-fried to produce crisp, golden fritters. It is a simple process, but make sure the fat is clean, for lingering smells in the oil can easily spoil the delicate flavour of the fruit.

Choux pastry is made in a completely different way from any other pastry, but the result is well worth a try. The flour is added to the liquid all at once to make a paste, and the air is beaten in with the eggs to give the characteristic light and airy texture to the cooked choux. If the end result appears 'cakey' you have beaten it too long at the first stage; if pale and flabby, the oven was too cool; if it sinks when taken out of the oven, it required longer cooking, and if it did not rise, perhaps you used self-raising flour by mistake. But take heart – practice makes perfect!

Do not be distracted by anything while you are deep fat frying. A pan alight is a very frightening and dangerous thing.

PANCAKE BATTER

Makes 10–12 pancakes

100 g (4 oz) plain flour
scant ¼ tsp salt
2 tsp caster sugar (optional)
1 egg
1 egg yolk
275 ml (½ pint) milk and water
  ie 225 ml (8 fl oz) milk and
  50 ml (2 fl oz) water
25 g (1 oz) very soft butter

Sieve the flour and salt into a bowl. Add the sugar if it is to be a sweet pancake. Make a deep well in the flour. Break the egg into it and add the egg yolk. Stir a little of the milk into the eggs with a wooden spoon. Continue to stir, gradually incorporating the flour and adding the milk as needed. When all is used up, beat until smooth for a minute or two. Then add the very soft, but not melted butter, and beat again. The batter should be a thin cream.

The batter should now rest for 1 hour. During this time the starch grains swell and are easily broken down in the brisk heat needed for successful pancake making. The use of a wooden spoon also helps to 'batter' the starch grains. This makes a light, beautifully textured pancake. This pancake mixture can be varied by increasing or reducing the amount of flour. Family pancakes can be made from a slightly thicker batter containing more flour. Party pancakes, light and lacy, can be made from a batter as thin as you dare.

Heat the pan and wipe it over with butter or oil. The fat is used not to fry the pancake but simply to stop it sticking.

A pancake pan is made of cast iron, about 12.5–18 cm (5–7 inches) across. It should never be washed, just wiped with an oily paper. From a properly cared-for pan, any child with a straight eye can toss a pancake.

SHROVE TUESDAY PANCAKES

Makes 10–12 pancakes

butter or oil
275 ml (½ pint) pancake batter (see page 46)
lemons
caster sugar

Heat the pan and add a little butter or oil. Pour in a tablespoon of batter and twist the pan so the base is evenly coated. Cook until beginning to bubble on top. Turn with a palette knife or toss over and cook the other side until lightly browned. Keep warm in a folded tea towel, or in the oven in a covered dish until all the pancakes are made.

Squeeze lemon juice liberally over each pancake. Dust with sugar. Roll up and serve at once with lemon wedges.

CHOUX PASTRY

220 ml (7½ fl oz) water
75 g (3 oz) butter
100 g (4 oz) plain flour, scant weight
3 eggs

Bring the water to the boil with the butter. Sieve the flour on to a piece of paper. Take the pan off the heat, shoot the flour in all at once and beat with a wooden spoon until smooth. Return to a moderate heat and beat until the mixture is just leaving the sides of the pan, but no longer (this is important). Cool.

Whisk the eggs really well. Add them to the mixture by degrees, beating all the time until smooth and glossy. The mixture has to be firm enough to hold its shape, so go easy with the last spoonful or so of egg in case it gets too slack.

Cook at temperatures indicated in the individual recipes.

This is a decorative party pastry, entirely French, attractive, crisp and very easy to make.

A forcing bag with a 5-mm (¼-inch) and a 1-cm (½-inch) tube (or pipe) is handy to have for piping out the choux into pretty shapes.

SWEET FRITTER BATTER

150 g (5 oz) plain flour
25 g (1 oz) caster sugar
2 eggs
1 tbsp butter
275 ml (½ pint) milk

Put the flour and sugar into a bowl. Make a well and drop one whole egg and the yolk of the second egg into it. Stir the eggs. Add the milk and draw down the flour by degrees, beating continuously until smooth. Soften the butter and beat in. Leave to stand for 1 hour. Just before using, whisk the egg white stiffly and fold it evenly through the batter.

PRALINE

100 g (4 oz) unblanched almonds
100 g (4 oz) caster sugar

Put the ingredients in a heavy-based pan over a very low heat. Cook, stirring constantly with a wooden spoon until the sugar melts. When the sugar starts turning colour, stir gently with a metal spoon until it turns a rich amber colour (but is not burnt). Pour into a well oiled tin and leave to cool. When the praline has set hard, break it into pieces and transfer to a polythene bag. Run a rolling pin over the praline until it is the consistency of biscuit crumbs.

Store in an absolutely airtight container. Praline will keep for several months.

CHOCOLATE SAUCE

100 g (4 oz) plain chocolate
150 ml (¼ pint) hot water
25 g (1 oz) sugar
50 g (2 oz) butter

Break up the chocolate and put it with the water and sugar in a bowl over hot water. Heat until melted, stirring all the time. Raise the heat and cook for a minute or two. Remove from the heat, gradually beat in the butter and leave to cool.

CRÊPES BRETONNES

Serves 4

100 g (4 oz) wholemeal flour
¼ tsp salt
1 egg
1 tbsp olive oil
275 ml (½ pint) milk and water
butter or oil for frying
lemon juice
sugar

Mix the flour and salt in a bowl. Make a well in the centre. Beat the egg and oil together and pour into the well. Draw down a little flour and stir. Pour the milk slowly into the egg mixture, continue to draw the flour down and beat well. Finally beat for 2 minutes. Leave to stand for 1 hour. Then add more milk if the mixture is too thick – it should be like thin cream.

Heat the pan and add a little butter or oil. Make the pancakes as for Shrove Tuesday pancakes (see page 47). Sprinkle with lemon juice and sugar and roll up. Serve side by side in a warm dish, with lemon wedges.

These are the buckweat pancakes sold to everyone who holidays in Brittany. With the upsurge of wholefood shops, buckwheat flour can sometimes be found. If not, use wholemeal as stated in the recipe.

APRICOT AND WALNUT PANCAKES

Makes 10–12

225-g (8-oz) can apricots
25 g (1 oz) walnut pieces
275 ml (½ pint) pancake batter (see page 46)
butter or oil for frying
a little caster sugar

Mash the apricots with a wooden salad fork. Stir in the walnut pieces.

Heat the pan and make the pancakes as for Shrove Tuesday pancakes (see page 47). Spread them with the apricot mixture and roll up. Dust with sugar and serve at once.

Homemade apricot jam is as good as, if not better than, canned apricots for the filling. Bought jam is *not*. Homemade jam of any kind makes a delicious filling for pancakes, with the addition of a few nuts or a spoonful of sherry.

RASPBERRY PANCAKES

Makes 10–12

275 ml (½ pint) pancake batter (see
   page 46)
100 g (4 oz) raspberry jam
   (preferably homemade)
50 g (2 oz) flaked almonds, toasted
150 ml (¼ pint) whipping cream

Heat the pan and make the pancakes as for Shrove Tuesday pancakes (see page 46). Spread with raspberry jam. Roll up and arrange side by side in an ovenproof dish. Sprinkle with the almonds and serve with lightly whipped cream.

The pancakes can be kept warm in a covered dish in a moderate oven 180°C (350°F) mark 4 for about 20 minutes.

ALMOND AND PEAR CRÊPES

Makes 10–12

275 ml (½ pint) pancake batter (see
   page 46)
1 tbsp brandy
butter or oil for frying
100 g (4 oz) butter
50 g (2 oz) icing sugar, sifted
50 g (2 oz) ground almonds
¼ tsp almond essence
425-g (15-oz) can pears or 4 fresh
   pears
25 g (1 oz) butter, melted (optional)
extra icing sugar

Stir the brandy into the butter. Heat the pan and make the pancakes as for Shrove Tuesday pancakes (see page 47).

Cream the butter and icing sugar together until light and fluffy. Stir in the ground almonds and essence. Peel, core and dice the pears and stir with the butter mixture. Spoon this mixture on to the pancakes, slightly to one side. Fold in half and then fold again to make triangles. Put in an ovenproof dish, dust with a little icing sugar and serve at once.

If the pancakes are to be kept warm in the oven, brush first with melted butter and then dust with icing sugar.

CRÊPES BEURRE AU CHOCOLAT

Makes 10–12

275 ml (½ pint) pancake batter (see page 46)
butter or oil for frying
175 g (6 oz) butter, softened
175 g (6 oz) dark plain chocolate

Make up the pancake mixture as before, but a little thinner. Heat the pan and make the pancakes as for Shrove Tuesday pancakes (see page 47). Keep warm in a folded tea towel (the garçons of Paris of course make them one at a time, on demand).

Spread the softened butter on the crêpes. Grate the chocolate and sprinkle it over the butter. Fold into four, put in a hot dish and serve at once.

Those of you who know Paris envy the skill of the garçons who so casually pour batter on to a hot-plate and produce a perfect crêpe every time, then fold it in four and hand it to you in a paper cornet. But the garçons know nothing about the best pancake in the world, our own lemon and sugar Shrove Tuesday pancake.

CRÊPES SUZETTE

Makes 8–10 pancakes

3 tbsp brandy
275 ml (½ pint) pancake batter (see page 46)
butter or oil for frying
50 g (2 oz) caster sugar
25 g (1 oz) butter
grated rind and juice of 2 oranges
1 tbsp Grand Marnier

Add 1 tablespoon of brandy to the batter. Heat the pan and make the pancakes as for Shrove Tuesday pancakes (see page 47). Keep hot. Melt the sugar slowly in a saucepan with 1 teaspoon of water (no more); heat until it caramelizes. Add the butter and the grated rind and juice of the oranges. Stir gently. Run the crêpes through this sauce and fold each into four. Put in an ovenproof dish. Add the Grand Marnier to the remaining sauce and pour over the crêpes. Heat the remaining brandy in a ladle over a candle flame at the table. Put a match to it and pour whilst flaming over the crêpes. Serve immediately.

CRÊPES PRALINÉES

Makes 10–12

275 ml (½ pint) pancake batter (see page 46)
50 g (2 oz) butter
50 g (2 oz) caster sugar
3 tbsp praline (see page 48)
1–2 tbsp rum (optional)

Heat the pan and make the pancakes as for Shrove Tuesday pancakes (see page 47). Keep warm.

Cream the butter and sugar until light and fluffy. Put a rolling pin over the praline to crush it. Fold the powdery result into the butter and add the rum if used. Spread on the crêpes, fold in four and serve at once.

BATTERED SANDWICHES

275 ml (½ pint) pancake batter (see page 46)
bread, butter and jam
margarine
caster sugar

Make jam sandwiches. Cut each into three pieces. Dip into the batter and fry in plenty of piping hot melted margarine. Dust with sugar and serve at once.

These were made, and no doubt invented, by a Hampshire countrywoman, and fed straight into the mouths of ten children who still remember them with love. They make a humble, homely but delicious contrast to their sophisticated equivalents from across the Channel, as does the following recipe.

SAUCER PANCAKES

275 ml (½ pint) pancake batter (see page 46)
raspberry or other jam

Heat the oven to 190°C (375°F) mark 5. Butter six saucers – large, comfortable, breakfast-sized ones. Divide the batter between them. Put a teaspoon of any jam into the middle of each and bake for 15–20 minutes.

SWEET YORKSHIRE PUDDING

Serves 4

100 g (4 oz) plain flour
¼ tsp salt
2 eggs (size 3 or 4)
200 ml (7 fl oz) milk and water,
    mixed
75 g (3 oz) butter
1 tbsp oil
golden syrup, warmed

Heat the oven to 220°C (425°F) mark 7.
Sieve the flour and salt into a bowl. Make a
well in the centre. Break the eggs into this,
or into a cup first if you are doubtful. Stir to
break the yolks. Add a little of the milk and
water and beat with a wooden spoon. Draw
down the flour by degrees, then add all the
liquid, beating to keep the batter smooth.
Beat for 2 minutes, then leave to stand for
30 minutes.

Put the butter and oil into a 20–23-cm
(8–9-inch) square baking tin and put into
the hot oven. When piping hot, pour the
batter into the hot fat. Cook for 45 minutes.
Pour melted syrup over it and serve at once.

COLLEGE PUDDING

Serves 4

100 g (4 oz) plain flour
¼ tsp salt
1–2 eggs
275 ml (½ pint) milk
50 g (2 oz) butter
2 tsp oil
450 g (1 lb) cooking apples
bramble jelly
75 g (3 oz) caster sugar

Heat the oven to 220°C (425°F) mark 7.
Make a batter by sifting the flour and salt
together. Beat the eggs and milk gradually
into it, until absolutely smooth. Leave to
stand for 30 minutes.

Heat the butter and oil in an ovenproof
casserole (the oil prevents the butter from
burning). Peel, core and slice the apples and
add them to the hot butter. Dot with
teaspoons of bramble jelly and sprinkle with
sugar. Give the batter a stir before pouring
it over the apples. Cook for about 1 hour or
until brown and risen. Serve at once, as
baked batters sink if kept waiting.

APRICOT FRITTERS

Serves 4

6 fresh ripe apricots
275 ml (½ pint) sweet fritter batter
  (see page 48)

Skin the apricots (dip them in boiling water), split and remove the stones. Dip each in the batter and fry as for apple fritters (see page 55) until honey brown. Drain on absorbent kitchen paper and serve in a hot dish with whipped cream.

PRUNE FRITTERS

Serves 4

15 prunes
½ glass red wine
1 cup strong tea (no milk)
15 unblanched almonds
25–40 g (1–1½ oz) mixed peel
275 ml (½ pint) sweet fritter batter
  (see page 48)
oil for frying

Stone the prunes and simmer in the wine and tea for 8–10 minutes. Stuff each prune with an unblanched almond and a little mixed peel. Pat dry with absorbent kitchen paper.

Dip each prune in the batter and fry as for apple fritters (see page 55). Serve immediately arranged in a hot dish dredged with caster sugar and with whipped cream.

CORN FRITTERS

Serves 4

100 g (4 oz) sweetcorn, frozen or
  canned
100 g (4 oz) plain flour
¼ tsp salt
1 egg
275 ml (½ pint) milk
50 g (2 oz) butter
oil
golden syrup

Thaw or drain the sweetcorn. Sieve the flour and salt into a bowl. Make a well in the centre and break the egg into it. Add a little milk. Beat again and gradually draw in the flour, beating in more milk until the mixture is creamy and smooth. Leave to stand for 1 hour.

Stir the corn into the batter. Heat the butter with a little oil in a frying pan. Drop teaspoonfuls of the mixture into the hot fat. Cook until lightly browned and cook the other side until golden. Drain on absorbent kitchen paper and serve very hot with golden syrup.

APPLE FRITTERS

Serves 4

*275 ml (½ pint) sweet fritter batter
  (see page 48)*
3 or 4 apples
caster sugar
ground cinnamon
oil for frying

Peel, core and cut the apples into rings 1 cm (½ inch) thick. Place them on a plate and sprinkle with caster sugar and cinnamon. Dip the rings in the batter – a skewer with the end turned up is a handy tool for this. Heat about 5 cm (2 inches) of oil in a deep frying pan to 190°C (375°F). Test the temperature by dropping a little of the batter into the oil: if the batter sizzles, the oil is hot enough.

Cook the rings a few at a time until golden brown on each side. Remove with a slotted spoon and drain on absorbent kitchen paper. Keep piping hot in the oven until all the fritters are ready. Arrange the fritters overlapping each other in a hot dish. Dust with caster sugar and serve immediately.

PROFITEROLES

Serves 4–6

100 g (4 oz) choux pastry (see page 47)
whipped cream
icing sugar
chocolate sauce (see page 48)

Heat the oven to 220°C (425°F) mark 7. Put the pastry into a forcing bag fitted with a 1.5-cm (1¾-inch) pipe. Pipe small rounds on to a baking sheet lined with non-stick baking paper. Leave about 4 cm (1½ inches) between the rounds to allow for them to expand. Cook until risen and golden brown – about 20 minutes. Pierce each bun to let the steam escape, and return to the oven for 5 minutes to dry out. Transfer to a wire rack.

When cold, pipe whipped cream into each choux ball using a forcing bag fitted with a 5-mm (¼-inch) pipe. Pile neatly on a serving dish or into individual glasses, dust lightly with icing sugar and pour chocolate sauce over them.

MERINGUES, MOUSSES AND SOUFFLÉS

This chapter contains an exciting range of
simple and more elaborate recipes for
meringues, hot and cold soufflés, and mousses
combined with fruits or other flavourings.

A cold soufflé has whisked egg whites folded into it just before it sets, regardless of the base, which may be custard or fruit purée. It is turned into a soufflé dish which has a stiff paper or foil 'collar' tied round it so when set, it may be removed to reveal the soufflé standing about 2.5 cm (1 inch) above the rim of the dish.

With a hot soufflé the base gives the flavour and the egg white the raising power. Fill the prepared dish not more than three-quarters full, and cook on a hot baking sheet towards the bottom of the oven – with nothing else in the oven. Keep the family waiting, for it sinks rapidly when removed from the oven. No collar is necessary for a hot soufflé.

A mousse is creamier and denser than a soufflé, usually containing more egg yolks and less, or sometimes no, whisked egg white. It is set into a bowl and, unlike a soufflé, never comes above the dish.

Meringues are everyone's favourites and there are several different ways of making them. Meringue cuite is the very firm one used for making meringue baskets and other shapes. *Cuite* means cooked – it isn't cooked, but is whisked over heat, which is probably how it acquired the name. Our everyday meringue is known as meringue suisse, and is suitable for individual meringues as well as for piping or spreading over various puddings or desserts which call for a meringue topping. Pavlova is the Australian meringue shell with the crisp outside and soft, gooey centre, made with the addition of vinegar and cornflour. Don't forget too, that soft brown sugar makes delicious meringues and does away with any problems of pale, coffee-coloured meringues – for they are that colour even before baking.

MERINGUE CUITE

4 egg whites
250 g (9 oz) icing sugar (flavoured
   with a vanilla pod)

If you use an electric whisk, all well and good. If not, whisk with the basin over a pan of hot water on a low heat. Put the whites with the sieved icing sugar into a warmed, dry bowl. Whisk them until very firm indeed.

Use a forcing bag fitted with a 1-cm (½-inch) pipe.

Use according to individual recipes.

MERINGUE SUISSE

2 egg whites
100 g (4 oz) caster sugar

Whisk egg whites very stiffly. Whisk in half the sugar, a little at a time, and then fold in the rest with a metal spoon. The meringue should be a velvety, dense mass, stiff enough to stay in the inverted bowl.

MERINGUE SHELLS

Makes 5–6 complete meringues

2 egg whites
100 g (4 oz) caster sugar
whipping cream

Heat the oven to 120°C (250°F) mark ½. Make the meringue suisse (as above) and shape the shells by taking a dessertspoon of the mixture and spooning it out with another dessertspoon. Do this until you achieve a smooth oval shape, then spoon it on to a baking sheet lined with non-stick paper. As the second dessertspoon comes away, tip a little tail over the top of the meringue. This is the classic shape.

Cook in a cool oven until firm, dry and set, about 2 hours, reversing the sheets in the oven after an hour. Sandwich together with firmly whipped cream.

BROWN SUGAR MERINGUES

2 egg whites
100 g (4 oz) soft light brown sugar

Heat the oven to 120°C (250°F) mark ½.
Make the meringue suisse (see page 58), but
use soft, light brown sugar instead
of caster. Whisk the egg whites a little longer
at both stages of whisking, and fold in the
remaining sugar in small amounts. Shape or
pipe on to baking sheets lined with
non-stick paper and cook for 2–2½ hours.
Use for any meringue suisse recipe. These
take a little longer to dry out.

APPLE SPONGE MERINGUE

Serves 4–5

150 g (5 oz) butter
250 g (9 oz) caster sugar
3 eggs
200 g (7 oz) self-raising flour
3 or 4 cooking apples
50 g (2 oz) caster sugar
¼ tsp ground cinnamon
2-egg white quantity of meringue
  suisse (see page 58)

Heat the oven to 160°C (325°F) mark 3.
Butter a 25-cm (10-inch) fluted ovenproof
china flan case or other ovenproof dish.
Cream the butter and sugar together
until light and fluffy. Add the eggs one at a
time and beat well. Fold in the sieved flour.
Turn into the flan case and cook for
40 minutes.

Peel, core and slice the apples, simmer
with the sugar and cinnamon in a very little
water until tender, then rub through a sieve
or mash. When the sponge base is cool,
spread the apple over the surface. Fill a
forcing bag fitted with a 2.5-cm (1-inch) star
pipe, and use to make circles of meringue
over the apple, or put it on with a spoon and
swirl with a fork. Cook for 1 hour until the
meringue is crisp.

STRAWBERRY VACHERIN

Serves 4–6

*4-egg white quantity of meringue
  cuite (see page 58)*
450 g (1 lb) strawberries
275 ml (½ pint) whipping cream

Heat the oven to 160°C (325°F) mark 3. Line a baking sheet with non-stick baking paper and draw a 15–18-cm (6–7-inch) circle on it. Put a sheet of rice paper over this. The pencil mark will show through. Fill a forcing bag fitted with a 2.5-cm (1-inch) pipe with meringue. With a spoon, put the remaining meringue on the rice paper to cover the whole circle about 1 cm (½ inch) deep. Smooth it with the spoon.

Holding the tube upright, pipe the first ring of your basket on to the meringue base around the edge but still on the meringue. Then pipe two more rings, one on top of the other, taking care to keep the 'walls' even.

Cook for 1½ hours or until really firm. Have the serving dish ready. Slip the vacherin case on to it – the rice paper comes easily away from the baking paper. When cold, trim the rice paper from the sides of the meringue with your fingers. Cut the strawberries in half. Dust them with sugar and reserve a few for decoration. Whip the cream until stiff, fold the strawberries into it and very gently pile into the case, putting the reserved strawberries on the top.

Serve reasonably soon after making.

A vacherin is a meringue case or basket. It is made with meringue cuite which is especially stiff and holds its shape well.

BAKED ALASKA

Serves 4–6

1 Victoria sandwich layer, 18 cm (7 inches) across
1 family block ice cream or 1 litre (1 quart) in a round tub (vanilla or any other flavour)
2-egg white quantity of meringue suisse (see page 58)

Heat the oven to 230°C (450°C) mark 8. Put the sponge cake on to an ovenproof plate. Turn the stiffly frozen ice cream on to the cake, keeping it in the centre. Use the meringue to completely mask the ice cream and cake, leaving no gaps at all. Cook in the centre of the oven for 4 minutes and serve at once.

Fruit may be placed under and around the ice cream for a change. Use a flavoured ice cream to blend with the fruit.

PAVLOVA

Serves 6–8

4 egg whites
225 g (8 oz) caster sugar
4 tsp cornflour
2 tsp white vinegar
275 ml (½ pint) whipping cream
4 fresh peaches

Heat the oven to 120°C (250°F) mark ½. Whisk the egg whites until stiff. Add the sugar, 2 tablespoons at a time, beating between each addition. When the sugar is used up, beat for 1–2 minutes until the meringue is dense, velvety and very, very stiff. Then beat in the cornflour, sprinkling it over the meringue, and finally the vinegar.

Butter an attractive, shallow ovenproof dish. Put the meringue into it, making a hollowish dip in the centre. Bake for 1½ hours at least until really firm and set. Whip the cream. Peel and slice the fresh peaches and fold into the cream. When the meringue is cooked, put the fruit into it. Serve without too much delay.

This is an Australian meringue. The addition of cornflour and vinegar give it a soft texture inside and a crisp outer crust. Fresh fruit really is best for this.

RASPBERRY MERINGUE PIE

Serves 4

1 Swiss roll
425-g (15-oz) can raspberries
2 egg white quantity of meringue suisse (see page 58)

Heat the oven to 180°C (350°F) mark 4. Cut the Swiss roll into slices. Arrange over the base and sides of a glass ovenproof dish. Spoon the raspberries and their juice over the sponge cake. Pile the meringue on top, swirling it attractively with a fork. Cook until the meringue is crisp, about 30 minutes. It will be soft inside.

RASPBERRY MERINGUE BASKETS

Makes about 6

4 egg white quantity of meringue cuite (see page 58)
225 g (½ lb) fresh raspberries
1 packet raspberry jelly

Heat the oven to 120°C (250°F) mark ½. Line two baking sheets with non-stick baking paper. Draw six circles about 7.5 cm (3 inches) across. Put rice paper over them. Fill a forcing bag fitted with a 1-cm (½-inch) plain pipe with as much meringue as you can comfortably handle (refill when you need more). Pipe six little baskets using the same method as for the big vacherin case (see page 60) – pipe a circle to cover the base and then build up the 'walls'. Cook for about 1½ hours or until firm and dry.

Make up the packet of jelly with 210 ml (7½ fl oz) water, cool until nearly set. Turn the fresh raspberries in this, reserving six for decoration. Remove the baskets from the oven. Slip them off the baking paper and trim away the spare rice paper. Put the basket on to a serving dish. When they are perfectly cold, fill with the jelly-covered raspberries. Top each with a reserved raspberry.

The raspberries should only be lightly jellied. Children like mandarin orange segments used in this pretty dessert. Dry the segments and use orange jelly.

CHOCOLATE MERINGUE CASTLE

Serves 6–8

*4 egg white quantity of meringue
  suisse (see page 58)*
275 ml (½ pint) whipping cream
100 g (4 oz) plain chocolate

Heat the oven to 120°C (250°F) mark ½.
Fill a forcing bag fitted with a large star pipe
with the meringue and use to make 24 stars,
piping on to baking sheets lined with
non-stick baking paper. Cook for about
1½ hours, until lightly coloured, reversing
trays in the oven after an hour. Cool.

Arrange a circle of stars closely together
on a decorative plate. Whip the cream stiffly
and pipe stars between and on top of the
meringues. Continue to build the meringue
with the cream into a pyramid shape, using
the stars as decoration. Melt the chocolate
in a bowl over hot water and spoon over the
castle from the top.

The chocolate sets hard and gives a
wonderful variety of textures in this cake.

HAZELNUT COFFEE MERINGUES

Makes about 10

*2-egg quantity meringue suisse (see
  page 58)*
*50 g (2 oz) hazelnuts,
  very finely chopped*
½ tsp instant coffee powder
150 ml (¼ pint) whipping cream

Heat the oven to 120°C (250°F) mark ½.
Make up the meringue suisse then fold in
the hazelnuts and 1 teaspoon of instant
coffee powder. Either pipe or make into
'shells' with dessertspoons (see page 58) on
to baking sheets lined with non-stick baking
paper, and cook for 2 hours at least,
reversing the sheets after 1 hour.

Whip the cream with the remaining
instant coffee until stiff, then use to
sandwich the meringues together.

LEMON SOUFFLÉ

Serves 4–6

175 g (6 oz) caster sugar
3 eggs, separated
grated rind and juice of 2 lemons
15 g (½-oz) powdered gelatine
3 tbsp water
175 ml (6 fl oz) whipping cream

Prepare a 575-ml (1-pint) soufflé dish, sometimes called a case, by tying a paper or foil cuff round it to come 2.5–5 cm (1–2 inches) above the rim. The cuff should be lightly oiled to make it easy to remove before serving.

Whisk the sugar with the egg yolks in a basin until light and fluffy. Add the rind and juice of the lemons to the eggs. Put the bowl over a pan of gently simmering water and whisk until the mixture is thick and creamy. (This is the most important part of making a cold soufflé.) Whisk, off the heat for a moment or two more. Cool.

Dissolve the gelatine in the water in a basin over hot water. Add to the mixture, pouring it in a thin stream. This prevents the gelatine from 'stringing'. Whisk the egg whites until just stiff. Lightly whip the cream. Fold the cream into the lemon mixture followed by the egg whites, very lightly and with a metal spoon. Pour the mixture into the dish and chill until set. Remove collar just before serving.

ORANGE SOUFFLÉ

Serves 4–6

3 eggs
2 egg yolks
25 g (1 oz) caster sugar
grated rind and juice of 2 oranges
15 g (½ oz) powdered gelatine
150 ml (¼ pint) whipping cream
2 glacé orange slices

Prepare the soufflé dish as for lemon Soufflé (see above). Break the eggs into a bowl and add the yolks with the sugar. Add the orange rind to the eggs. Whisk over a pan of hot water until thick. Take off the heat and whisk until cool.

Dissolve the gelatine in the orange juice in a bowl over hot water. Make up to 175 ml (6 fl oz) with water or pure canned orange juice. Whisk into the mixture and leave until on the point of setting. Lightly whip the cream and fold in. Pour into a dish and chill until set.

Remove the collar and decorate with quartered glacé orange slices.

This soufflé is made by a different method, called Milanese.

GINGER SOUFFLÉ

Serves 4–6

425 ml (¾ pint) milk
3 eggs, separated
50 g (2 oz) caster sugar
2 tbsp ginger syrup
15 g (½ oz) powdered gelatine
50 g (2 oz) stem ginger, sliced
150 ml (¼ pint) whipping cream
extra whipped cream and stem
*   ginger to decorate*

Prepare an 850-ml (1½-pint) soufflé dish as for lemon soufflé (see page 64). Boil the milk. Beat the egg yolks and sugar together until pale. Add the ginger syrup. Pour the milk on to the eggs, beating all the time. Return to the pan and heat gently, stirring all the time until the mixture thickens. Dissolve the gelatine in 2 tablespoons of water in a basin over hot water. Add to the mixture. Stir well and cool. Fold in the sliced stem ginger.

When almost at setting point, whisk the egg whites firmly and whip the cream lightly. Fold the cream into the mixture followed by the egg whites, using a metal spoon. Pour into the dish and leave until it is set.

Remove the collar and decorate with whipped cream and a few slices of stem ginger.

This soufflé can also be made with a good ginger wine and crystallised ginger.

HOT BANANA SOUFFLÉ

Serves 4–6

*4 bananas, not more than 450 g
  (1 lb) unpeeled weight
grated rind and juice of 1 orange
grated rind and juice of 1 lemon
75 g (3 oz) caster sugar
25 g (1 oz) walnut pieces, chopped
3 egg whites
pinch of salt*

Prepare an 18–20-cm (7–8-inch) soufflé dish by buttering it well. Heat the oven to 180°C (350°F) mark 4, with a baking sheet in it.

Peel and mash the bananas. Add the lemon and orange juice and rind to the bananas with the sugar and nuts. Whisk the egg whites until stiff with a pinch of salt. Fold into the banana purée and turn into the dish. Stand the dish on the baking sheet in the lower half of the oven and cook at once for 30 minutes. The top of the dish should be at the middle line in the oven. Serve immediately.

HOT CHOCOLATE SOUFFLÉ

Serves 4–6

*100 g (4 oz) good dark block
  chocolate
2 tbsp water
425 ml (¾ pint) milk
50 g (2 oz) vanilla sugar (keep a
  pod in the sugar jar)
40 g (1½ oz) arrowroot
15 g (½ oz) butter
3 eggs
1 egg white
icing sugar*

Butter a 1-litre (2-pint) soufflé dish. Heat the oven to 190°C (375°F) mark 5 with a baking sheet in it.

Melt the chocolate with the water over a gentle heat. Heat the milk in a large pan, keeping back 50 ml (2 fl oz), and dissolve the sugar in it. Pour the melted chocolate into the milk and mix well. Blend the arrowroot with the remaining milk. Pour some of the hot chocolate mixture on to it, stir well, return to the saucepan and bring to the boil, stirring continuously. Remove from the heat, dot with the butter, cover the pan and cool.

Separate the eggs and beat the egg yolks into the cooled mixture, one at a time. Whisk the whites stiffly and fold in with a metal spoon. Turn into the dish. Stand on the baking sheet and cook for 20–30 minutes. Serve immediately.

HOT LEMON SOUFFLÉ

Serves 4–6

40 g (1½ oz) butter
40 g (1½ oz) plain flour
425 ml (¾ pint) milk
50 g (2 oz) caster sugar
grated rind and juice of 2 lemons
3 eggs, separated
icing sugar

Prepare an 18–20-cm (7–8-inch) soufflé dish by buttering it well. Heat the oven to 190°C (375°F) mark 5 with a baking sheet in it.

Melt the butter in a large pan. Remove from the heat and stir in the flour. Put back on the heat and gradually add the milk, stirring all the time until boiling. Remove from the heat, add the sugar, grated rind and juice of the lemons and beat well.

Beat in the egg yolks one at a time. Whisk the whites stiffly and fold into the mixture with a metal spoon. Pour into the dish and cook, standing the dish on the baking sheet, for 30 minutes. When cooked, dust the top very quickly with a little icing sugar and serve immediately.

HOT VANILLA SOUFFLÉ

Serves 4–6

275 ml (½ pint) milk
1 vanilla pod
50 g (2 oz) vanilla flavoured sugar
5 eggs
40 g (1½ oz) plain flour
a little icing sugar

Prepare a soufflé dish by buttering it well. Heat the oven to 190°C (375°F) mark 5 with a baking sheet in it. Simmer the milk and vanilla pod together. Cream the sugar with one egg and an egg yolk until pale and very fluffy. Sieve the flour and stir in. Remove the pod from the milk. Pour the hot milk on to the egg mixture, stirring all the time. Return to the heat and cook gently, stirring continuously, until thick and smooth. Cover and cool.

Separate the remaining eggs. Beat the yolks into the cooled vanilla cream, one at a time. Whisk the egg whites firmly and fold into the mixture with a metal spoon. Turn into the dish, stand it on the baking sheet and cook for 30 minutes. When cooked, dust with a little icing sugar. Serve immediately.

RASPBERRY MOUSSE

Serves 6–8

900 g (2 lb) raspberries
175 g (6 oz) caster sugar
1 tbsp lemon juice
25 g (1 oz) powdered gelatine
4 tbsp water
275 ml (½ pint) whipping cream

Pick over the raspberries and reserve 6 or 7 for decoration. Mash the remainder with the sugar and lemon juice. A wooden salad fork is good for this. Dissolve the gelatine in the water in a bowl over hot water. Pour into the raspberries in a thin stream, folding as you pour.

Whip the cream until thick but not too stiff and fold it through the raspberries with a metal spoon. Pour into a dish and leave to set in the refrigerator.

Take the mousse out of the refrigerator 1 hour before serving, as intense cold masks the flavour. Decorate with the reserved raspberries.

There are no eggs in this mousse.

BRAMBLE MOUSSE

Serves 4–6

450 g (1 lb) blackberries
225 g (½ lb) cooking apples
75 g (3 oz) caster sugar
3 eggs
grated rind and juice of 1 lemon
15 g (½ oz) powdered gelatine
150 ml (¼ pint) whipping cream

Pick the blackberries over. Peel, core and slice the apples. Put all the fruit into a pan with 25 g (1 oz) sugar and cook over a very gentle heat until the juice has run and the fruit is soft. Sieve and cool.

Whisk the eggs with 50 g (2 oz) sugar over a pan of hot water until the mixture is thick and creamy. Cool a little. Grate the rind and squeeze the juice of the lemon. Dissolve the gelatine in the lemon juice in a bowl over hot water. Add the rind to the fruit purée and fold in the liquid gelatine. Whip the cream. Fold the egg mixture through the purée followed by the cream. Pour into a dish and chill until set.

APRICOT MOUSSE

Serves 4

170-g (6-fl oz) can evaporated milk
15-g (½-oz) powdered gelatine
425-g (15-oz) can apricots
3 eggs
50 g (2 oz) caster sugar
25 g (1 oz) toasted flaked almonds

Chill the unopened can of milk for 24 hours. Dissolve the gelatine in 2 tablespoons of water in a bowl over hot water. Purée the apricots in the blender or rub through a sieve. Beat the eggs with the sugar until light and fluffy, then fold into the purée. Fold in the gelatine, pouring in a thin stream. Whip the evaporated milk until thick and fold in. Pour into a dish and chill until set.

Sprinkle the top with toasted, flaked almonds before serving.

This simple recipe can be followed using 275 ml (½ pint) of any fruit purée, even apple.

CHOCOLATE AND ORANGE MOUSSE

Serves 4–5

175 g (6 oz) dark chocolate
3 tbsp black coffee
15 g (½ oz) butter
grated rind and juice of 2 oranges
3 eggs, separated

Melt the chocolate with the coffee in a bowl over hot water. Stir in the butter and remove from the heat. Grate the rind and squeeze the juice from the oranges. Separate the eggs and beat the yolks into the warm chocolate mixture one at a time, together with the orange rind and juice.

Whisk the egg whites stiffly and fold quickly into the mousse. Pour into a 15–17-cm (6–7-inch) dish. Leave to set in the refrigerator.

There is no gelatine in this mousse as the chocolate and eggs set it.

DESSERT GÂTEAUX

All gâteaux make an impressive dessert and are usually prepared, or at least part prepared well in advance, to leave the cook plenty of time to put the finishing touches to the dinner party.

Many gâteaux are sponge-based, created with layers of feather-light génoise sponge (borrowed from the French) and filled with creamy mixtures, often containing chocolate or fruit. Some gâteaux are completely masked with whipped cream or some form of crème, and may then have the sides coated in chopped nuts or grated chocolate. Others are left plain or may be topped with glacé icing or jam glaze.

All sponge cakes freeze perfectly and are immensely useful to have at hand for cakes such as the ones in this chapter. Thaw before filling and decorating.

Not all gâteaux are sponge-based. Some have layers of puff pastry, others, like sacher torte have their own special type of baked layers. Meringue and delicate sweet pastry layers are also featured.

Don't be put off by the thought of the various stages necessary in gâteaux making. They are really quite simple, and before you know it, an elegant gâteau will be in front of you.

GÉNOISE SPONGE CAKE

4 eggs
115 g (4½ oz) caster sugar
90 g (3½ oz) best fine white plain flour
90 g (3½ oz) butter (butter is a must)

Heat the oven to 180°C (350°F) mark 4. Prepare a 20-cm (8-inch) cake tin. Oil it lightly, line it carefully with baking paper and oil that too.

Break the eggs into a bowl, add the sugar and whisk over hot water until the mixture has almost doubled in bulk and the whisk leaves a heavy trail. Take off the heat and continue to whisk for a minute or two. Sift the flour twice to incorporate as much air as possible. Melt the butter and cool until just running. Fold the flour into the mixture with the melted butter. Mix swiftly but gently. Turn into the prepared tin and cook for 20–30 minutes until the cake is just shrinking from the sides of the tin. Turn out on to a cloth, invert on to a wire rack and leave to cool.

This is a lighter, French version of our English Victoria sponge, and is the perfect base for many gâteaux and petits fours.

CRÈME AU BEURRE MOUSSELINE (chocolat)

75 g (3 oz) granulated sugar
75 ml (3 fl oz) water
2 egg yolks
100 g (4 oz) butter
2 tbsp dark chocolate, melted

Put the sugar into the water. Melt completely and boil until syrupy (a short thread, to those of you who make sweets). Take off the heat at once. Whisk the yolks and pour the sugar on to them in a thin stream, whisking all the time. Whisk until thick and spongy. Beat the butter until it is very soft and creamy, then whisk into the spongy egg mixture by degrees. Melt the chocolate in a basin over hot water and gradually whisk into the crème. For a plain crème au beurre mousseline, omit the chocolate.

CRÈME AU BEURRE À LA MERINGUE

2 egg whites
*00 g (4 oz) icing sugar
*25 g (8 oz) butter, softened

Put the egg whites and sieved icing sugar into a basin over hot water. Beat until stiffly standing up in peaks. Take off the heat and beat until *absolutely* cold. Add the butter, whisking it in a little at a time.

CHOCOLATE ICING

*00 g (4 oz) cooking chocolate
tbsp water
*5 g (3 oz) sieved icing sugar

Melt the chocolate with the water in a bowl over a pan of hot water. Stir in the icing sugar until smooth and pour over the cake.

CHOCOLATE MARQUISE

*75 g (6 oz) good dark chocolate
tbsp strong black coffee
*5 g (1 oz) butter

Melt the chocolate with the coffee in a bowl over hot water, then beat in the butter. Use at once to spread over the cake.

GLACÉ ICING

*75 g (6 oz) icing sugar
*arm water

Sieve the icing sugar and gradually add 1 tbsp warm water to start with. Add more water in very small quantities to give a thick coating consistency. Add flavouring or colouring very sparingly, if liked.

MOCK FONDANT ICING

tsp liquid glucose
tsp warm water
*ing sugar

Dissolve the glucose in the water. Add sufficient icing sugar to give a coating consistency. Beat well. Colour or flavour as desired. Use at once.

GÂTEAU CARDINAL

Serves 6–8

crème au beurre à la meringue (see
  page 73)
20-cm (8-inch) baked round génoise
  sponge (see page 72)
50 g (2 oz) glacé cherries
2 tbsp kirsch
3 tbsp nuts, finely chopped
100 g (4 oz) redcurrant jelly

Keep back 4 or 5 tablespoons of the crème
au beurre à la meringue for decoration.
Chop the cherries and fold them with the
kirsch into the rest of the crème. Split the
cake in half and spread lavishly with the
filling. Reassemble.

Spread some of the reserved crème
around the sides of the cake. Put the
chopped nuts on to greaseproof paper and
roll the cake like a wheel across them to
decorate the sides. Stand on a serving plate.
Melt the redcurrant jelly. Spoon carefully
on to the top of the cake and leave to set.
Put the rest of the crème into a forcing bag
fitted with a small star pipe and work a neat
shell pattern around the edge of the jelly.

You may have seen this delicious cake in
Boulogne, where it is a speciality.

GÂTEAU ST GEORGES

Serves 4–6

4-egg recipe quantity of génoise
  sponge (see page 72)
100 g (4 oz) dark chocolate
2 eggs, separated
2 tsp rum
50 g (2 oz) butter, softened
100 g (4 oz) caster sugar

Prepare a 20–23-cm (8–9-inch) sponge flan
tin. Oil it well, put a round of baking paper
on to the bottom and oil again. Heat
the oven to 180°C (350°F) mark 4.

Pour the génoise mixture into the tin and
cook for 20–30 minutes until the cake starts
to shrink away from the sides of the tin.
Turn out and leave to cool.

Melt the chocolate with 1 tablespoon of
water in a basin over a pan of hot water.
When completely melted, remove from the
heat. Beat the egg yolks, one at a time, into
the chocolate with the butter and the rum.
When the butter is completely absorbed,
pour into the sponge flan case. Leave to set.
Heat the oven to 160°C (325°F) mark 3. Use

the egg whites and caster sugar to make a stiff meringue suisse (see page 58). Swirl the meringue on to the set chocolate and cook until set on the outside, about 20 minutes. It need not dry out like shells, but must be firmly set on top. Serve cold.

A wooden spoon is too thick for any folding operation. The thin edge of a metal spoon cuts through mixtures without breaking down the airy texture.

GÂTEAU MARGOT

erves 12

00 g (4 oz) plain flour
¼ tsp salt
eggs
75 g (6 oz) caster sugar
50 g (1 lb) strawberries
tbsp caster sugar
00 g (4 oz) good dark chocolate
75 ml (½ pint) whipping cream

Oil a ring mould, approximately 1.75 litres (3 pints). Heat the oven to 190°C (375°F) mark 5. Sieve the flour and salt together.

Whisk the eggs and 175 g (6 oz) sugar in a bowl over a pan of hot water until thick. Take off the heat and whisk until cold. Fold in the flour with a metal spoon and turn into the prepared tin. Cook for 35–40 minutes, then turn out on to a wire rack to cool.

For the filling, take 175 g (6 oz) strawberries, blend them with 1 tablespoon of sugar (or rub through a sieve or mash them). Melt the chocolate in a basin over hot water. Cut the cake across into three layers. Spread each layer with chocolate and leave to set.

Whip the cream stiffly, fold one-third into the strawberry purée and use to spread over the chocolate on each layer. Reassemble the cake and stand on a serving plate. Use the rest of the whipped cream to completely mask the cake, spreading with a palette knife. Fill the centre with the rest of the strawberries.

HAZELNUT GALETTE

Serves 4–6

100 g (4 oz) plain flour
pinch of salt
75 g (3 oz) butter
50 g (2 oz) sugar
75 g (3 oz) ground hazelnuts
6–8 apricot halves, fresh or canned
150 ml (¼ pint) whipping cream
icing sugar

Heat the oven to 180°C (350°F) mark 4. Line three baking sheets with baking paper. Sieve the flour with the salt. Make a well for the butter and sugar and sprinkle in the nuts. Draw the flour gradually into the middle, mixing with the fingertips until you have a firm, smooth dough. Wrap and chill for 20 minutes.

Divide the dough into three. Roll each piece into a circle about 15 cm (6 inches) across. Put the circles on the baking paper. Cook for about 20 minutes until golden brown. Remove carefully and cool on wire racks.

Chop the apricots. Whip the cream stiffly and fold into the apricots; use to sandwich the galette together. Dredge the top with icing sugar and serve fairly quickly.

A galette is a French Twelfth Cake, usually made with flaky pastry and traditionally eaten on Twelfth Night in the provinces north of the Loire. It has come to be used in English cookery, as rounds of pastry of various types with a rich filling.

FRENCH CHOCOLATE CAKE

Serves 4

50 g (2 oz) unsalted butter
100 g (4 oz) good dark chocolate
3 eggs, separated
50 g (2 oz) caster sugar
2 tsp plain flour
50 g (2 oz) ground almonds

Oil a 15–18-cm (6–7-inch) round cake tin, line with baking paper and oil again. Heat the oven to 180°C (350°F) mark 4. Soften the butter. Melt the chocolate in a basin over hot water and separate the eggs. Beat the butter and egg yolks into the chocolate. Fold in the sugar, flour and ground almonds. Whisk the egg whites very stiffly and fold into the chocolate mixture with a metal spoon. Turn into the prepared tin and

cook for about 45 minutes. Turn on to a
wire rack and leave to cool.

This is a small, rich, utterly French cake
which can be eaten plain or with a good
chocolate icing poured over it. Alternatively
it can be masked with whipped cream.

ACHER TORTE

rves 4–6

g (3 oz) good dark chocolate
bsp rum
g (3½ oz) butter
0 g (5 oz) caster sugar
·ggs (size 1 or 2), separated
g (3½ oz) unblanched hazelnuts,
ground
g (1½ oz) fresh white
breadcrumbs, dried
tsp powdered cloves
)colate icing (see page 73)

Heat the oven to 200°C (400°F) mark 6.
Melt the chocolate and rum in a bowl over
hot water. Grease and line a 23-cm (9-inch)
straight-sided sandwich tin with non-stick
baking parchment with the side band
coming 5 cm (2 inches) above the rim, and
grease again.

Cream the butter and sugar until light
and fluffy. Separate the eggs. Beat in the
egg yolks one at a time, then fold the
chocolate and rum into the mixture with a
metal spoon. Fold in the ground hazelnuts,
the breadcrumbs and the cloves.

Stiffly whisk the egg whites (which
should never be kept waiting) and fold them
into the mixture. Turn into the prepared tin
and cook until firm to the touch – about
30 minutes. Turn on to a wire rack and
leave to cool. When cold, cover with
chocolate icing. Serve with whipped cream.

There is no flour in this cake.

NUSSKUCHEN

Serves 6

75 g (3 oz) butter
75 g (3 oz) caster sugar
1 egg
50 g (2 oz) unblanched hazelnuts, ground
75 g (3 oz) plain flour
1 tsp instant coffee powder
2 tbsp milk
1 tsp baking powder
1 egg white
150 ml (¼ pint) whipping cream
450 g (1 lb) cooking apples
grated rind and juice of 1 lemon
50 g (2 oz) apricot jam
chocolate marquise (see page 73)

Oil and line a 20-cm (8-inch) deep sandwich tin and oil again. Heat the oven to 190°C (375°F) mark 5. Cream the butter and sugar until light and fluffy. Beat in the egg, nuts and sieved flour followed by the coffee and milk. Beat again. Fold in the baking powder and the stiffly beaten egg white. Turn into the prepared tin and cook for 20 minutes. Turn out on to a wire rack and leave to cool

Peel, core and slice the apples. Simmer with the grated rind and juice of the lemon and the apricot jam until soft, then cool.

Split the cake in half and sandwich together with the apple mixture. Cover the whole cake with chocolate marquise and serve fairly soon after it has set.

STRAWBERRY CREAM CAKE

Serves 6–8

1 recipe quantity génoise sponge (see page 72)
crème au beurre mousseline – plain (see page 72)
175 g (6 oz) strawberries
glacé icing (see page 73)
crystallised violets

Oil and line a 20–23-cm (8–9-inch) round cake tin with baking paper, then oil again. Heat the oven to 180°C (350°F) mark 4. Cook the mixture in the prepared tin for about 20–25 minutes. Turn out and cool on a wire rack. When cold, split carefully into three layers.

Make the crème au beurre mousseline, but without the chocolate. Crush the strawberries and fold into the crème. This makes a bulky filling. Spread over the layers of cake and reassemble. Pour white, or the very palest pink, glacé icing all over the cake. You may need a second coat. Move when the icing is cold and set the cake on to its serving plate.

Decorate with an informal group of real crystallised violets on the top. Wait until the icing has set or the colour will run.

TARTE AU CITRON

Serves 6

½ recipe quantity *pâte sucrée* (see page 16)
50 g (2 oz) caster sugar
egg
50 g (2 oz) ground almonds
lemons
275 ml (½ pint) water
vanilla pod
300 g (10 oz) granulated sugar
few angelica leaves

Heat the oven to 200°C (400°F) mark 6. Roll out the pastry and use it to line an 18–20-cm (7–8-inch) plate. Decorate the edge with the tip of a teaspoon.

Prepare the almond cream: add the caster sugar to the egg with the ground almonds and the grated rind of 1 lemon. Beat really well. Spread over the base of the pastry and cook for 25 minutes.

For the glazed lemon slices, slice the other 2 lemons thinly and poach until quite soft in the water with the vanilla pod added. Remove with a slotted spoon. Make the water up to 275 ml (½ pint) again and add the granulated sugar. Heat to dissolve the sugar then replace the lemon slices. Poach gently for 20 minutes. Remove the slices and place on a baking sheet or flat plate. Reduce the syrup until thick, cool and use to brush over the top of the tart. Arrange the lemon slices as attractively as possible on the tart and spoon the syrup sparingly over them. Put a *few* little diamonds of angelica around the edge like leaves.

GÂTEAU MILLES FEUILLES

Serves 6–8

350 g (¾ lb) bought puff pastry (frozen or chilled)
225 g (½ lb) raspberries
150 ml (¼ pint) whipping cream
little glacé icing (see page 73)

Heat the oven to 220°C (425°F) mark 7. Roll out the pastry thinly and cut into fine 18-cm (7-inch) rounds using a plate as a guide. Prick them well and place on baking sheets lined with non-stick baking paper. Cook for about 20 minutes until well puffed up and golden brown. Cool on wire racks.

When all are cold, sandwich together lightly with crushed raspberries folded into the whipped cream. Decorate the top with a little glacé icing.

AUSTRIAN CHEESECAKE

Serves 6–8

175 g (6 oz) digestive biscuits
75 g (3 oz) butter, melted
1 tsp ground cinnamon
450 g (1 lb) cream cheese
2 eggs
150 g (5 oz) caster sugar
grated rind and juice of 1 lemon
150 ml (¼ pint) soured cream
hazelnuts and maraschino cherries

Heat the oven to 190°C (375°F) mark 5.
Crush the biscuits in a polythene bag with a
rolling pin. Put the crumbs into a bowl with
the butter and cinnamon and mix well.
Press into the bottom and up the sides of a
20–23-cm (8–9-inch) fluted china
ovenproof flan dish. Neaten the top.

Beat the cheese until smooth. Whisk the
eggs with 75 g (3 oz) of the sugar until light
and fluffy. Fold into the cheese with the
grated rind and juice of the lemon. Pour on
to the biscuit base and cook for 30 minutes.

Remove from the oven, then increase the
oven temperature to 240°C (475°F) mark 9.

Mix the soured cream (you can sour fresh
cream with 1 tablespoon of lemon juice)
with the remaining 25 g (1 oz) of sugar.
Spoon on to the cake and return to a very
hot oven for 10 minutes. Cool and chill.

Take out of the refrigerator about an hour
before you need it and decorate the top with
two straight lines of hazelnuts, with a line of
maraschino cherries between them.

ANGEL CAKE WITH GRAPES

Serves 6–8

50 g (2 oz) plain flour
175 g (6 oz) caster sugar
6 egg whites
pinch of salt
¾ tsp cream of tartar
2 drops (but no more) vanilla
  essence (not flavouring)
1 drop almond essence
275 ml (½ pint) whipping cream
450 g (1 lb) green grapes

Heat the oven to 190°C (375°F) mark 5.
Have a ring mould, 20–23 cm (8–9 inches)
across ready, but do not grease it.

Sieve the flour and 75 g (3 oz) sugar at
least twice. Put the egg whites, salt and
cream of tartar into a large basin – dry and
polished. Whisk until the mixture is foamy.
Add the remaining sugar a little at a time
and whisk until very stiff and dense. Add
the essences and whisk again. Fold in the
flour with a metal spoon. Spoon into the dry
cake tin.

Cook the cake for 30–35 minutes until no
dent is made on its surface by a light finger.
Turn the whole tin upside down on a wire
rack. Cool. The cake will then drop out.
Lightly whip the cream and use to mask
the very delicate cake. Fill the centre with
skinned and de-pipped grapes.

DOBEZ TORTE

Serves 6–8

4 eggs
175 g (6 oz) caster sugar
150 g (5 oz) plain flour
175 g (6 oz) granulated sugar
2 recipe quantity crème au beurre
    mousseline chocolat (see page 72)
75 g (3 oz) good, dark chocolate,
    grated

Mark five circles on the underside of
non-stick baking paper about 20 cm
(8 inches) across. Lightly oil and put on to
baking sheets. Heat the oven to 180°C
(350°F) mark 4.

Whisk the eggs in a bowl over hot water,
adding the sugar by degrees until thick.
Fold in the sieved flour with a metal spoon.
Spoon and smooth on to the circles. Bake
until golden brown, about 15–20 minutes.

When cooked, carefully remove from the
paper and cool on wire racks (you need lots
of room and may have to bake in two
batches). Trim the edges neatly – a
saucepan lid may do the trick. Choose the
best one for the top. Melt the sugar with
4 tablespoons water in a heavy-based pan
and cook until caramel coloured, and then
pour over the top layer. When just about
to set, mark into sections with the back of
a knife.

Spread the other four pieces liberally with
the chocolate cream and sandwich lightly
together placing the caramel layer on top.
Spread the sides evenly with the crème and
press grated chocolate on to the sides. Pipe
neat rosettes of crème to neaten off the
caramelised edge.

GÂTEAU ALLEMAND

Serves 4–6

4 eggs
175 g (6 oz) caster sugar
grated rind and juice of 1 lemon
75 g (3 oz) semolina
25 g (1 oz) ground almonds
100 g (4 oz) homemade raspberry
  jam
150 ml (¼ pint) whipping cream
a little glacé icing (see page 73)
pink or green food colouring

Lightly oil a 20-cm (8-inch) square cake tin. Line the base with baking paper and oil again. Heat the oven to 190°C (375°F) mark 5.

Separate the eggs. Beat the yolks and sugar together until thick. Add the rind and juice of the lemon, the semolina and the ground almonds. Mix well. Whisk the egg whites stiffly and fold into the mixture. Turn into the tin and cook for 20–30 minutes.

Turn out on to a wire rack and leave to cool. Split the cake in half carefully. Spread one half with plenty of raspberry jam and whipped cream, and put the other half on top very lightly. Coat the top thinly with glacé icing, tinted pale pink or green with liquid food coloring. Leave to set.

GÂTEAU CITRON

Serves 6–8

1 recipe quantity génoise sponge
  baked in an 18-cm (7-inch) square
  tin (see page 72)
crème au beurre mousselin – plain
  (see page 72)
3 lemons
approx. 175 g (6 oz) icing sugar
yellow food colouring
40 g (1½ oz) granulated sugar

Split the cake into three layers. Make the crème as on page 72, but without the chocolate. Grate the rind and squeeze the juice of 2 lemons. Beat the grated rind of 1 lemon into the crème.

Spread the sponge layers with two-thirds of the crème and reassemble the cake. Reserve a little crème for piping and spread the sides of the cake with the remainder, using a small palette knife.

Make a lemon glacé icing with the sieved icing sugar and lemon juice. Beat in the grated rind of the second lemon and tint the palest yellow with food colouring. Carefully spread over the top of the cake and leave to set. Pipe small rosettes of the crème, or a shell pattern if you prefer, around the edge

to neaten its appearance.
Cut six thin slices from the remaining
lemon and remove the pips. Poach them
gently in a little water until the rind is
almost transparent. Remove carefully. Add
the granulated sugar to the water – about
50–75 ml (2–3 fl oz) by now – and stir until
completely dissolved. Put the slices back
and simmer for 5 minutes over a very low
heat. Lift the slices on to a wire rack over a
basin. Reduce the syrup without darkening,
pour over and leave to set.

Complete the decoration of the gâteau
with a diagonal row of these overlapping
glazed lemon slices.

APRICOT GÉNOISE CAKE

Serves 6

*génoise sponge cake baked in a
20-cm (8-inch) round tin (see
page 72)
450 g (1 lb) apricot jam, approx
fondant icing (see page 73)
50 g (2 oz) toasted, chopped
almonds*

Split the génoise cake horizontally into
three layers. Rub the apricot jam through a
sieve. Spread a layer of jam on one layer of
cake, cover with the middle layer, spread
this with jam too, and set the last layer on
top. Adjust to fit neatly.

Cover the top and sides of the cake with
apricot jam. Ice it with a fondant icing to
which you have added a few drops of kirsch
and sprinkle with chopped, browned
almonds if liked. Leave to set.

Contrary to what most people think,
gâteaux can be quite simple to make and
this one is a good example.

PARTY SPECIALS

After all the glamorous gâteaux, here is a chapter on equally spectacular desserts, but in a different vein. Cool and elegant concoctions served in pretty glasses, on delicate plates and even in their own shells, to bring a splendid ending to any dinner party.

Ice creams and sorbets are much easier to make than is generally thought, and they taste so good. They can form the base of many desserts, from pêche melba to the interesting brown bread ice cream. They also keep well in a freezer for several months.

Fruits feature here too, with the well-named raspberry flummery, ideal to make when there is a glut of soft fruit; or there is the famous strawberry romanoff and one of the most refreshing of all desserts – oranges in caramel.

Mostly simple to prepare and make, those desserts needing a little more time also require to be made in advance, so you can always provide something really splendid on those special occasions.

VANILLA ICE CREAM

Serves 6–8

175 g (6 oz) caster sugar
150 ml (¼ pint) water
5 egg yolks
275 ml (½ pint) whipping cream

Dissolve every grain of the sugar in the water over a gentle heat. Bring to the boil and boil fast for 5 minutes. Cool slightly. Beat the egg yolks. Pour the sugar syrup on to the yolks in a thin stream, beating all the time. Put the bowl over a saucepan of hot water and whisk until the mixture is thick. Leave until cold.

Whip the cream until stiff and fold into the mixture. Turn into a container, cover and freeze. When just beginning to set, remove to a bowl and beat hard again. This breaks down tiny ice crystals. Put back to freeze until completely firm.

Homemade ice cream is usually harder than the bought variety, so bring it out of the freezer about 15 minutes before you need it.

COFFEE ICE CREAM

Serves 6–8

175 g (6 oz) caster sugar
150 ml (¼ pint) water
5 gg yolks
150 ml (¼ pint) whipping cream
1½ tbsp instant coffee powder

Make as for vanilla ice cream (see page 85) but add the coffee with cream.

BROWN BREAD ICE CREAM

Serves 4–6

3 tbsp fresh brown breadcrumbs
1 tbsp caster sugar
600 ml (1 pint) vanilla ice cream
(see page 85)

Heat the oven to 180°C (350°F) mark 4. Put the breadcrumbs on a baking sheet and sprinkle them with caster sugar. Brown slowly in the oven for about 30 minutes or until really brown (but not burnt). Remove and cool. Beat into the still frozen ice cream and return to the freezer until needed.

The contrast of crumbs and creamy ice in this dish is delicious.

GOOSEBERRY ICE CREAM

Serves 6

450 g (1 lb) gooseberries
3 tbsp water
1 vanilla pod
3 tbsp caster sugar
1 tbsp packet custard powder
265 ml (½ pint) milk
1 egg
150 ml (¼ pint) whipping cream
green food colouring (optional)

Top, tail and wash the gooseberries. Simmer them in the water with the vanilla pod and 1 tablespoon caster sugar, until tender. Remove the pod and sieve the fruit.
Make the custard using the custard powder, milk and the rest of the sugar according to the instruction on the packet. Leave to cool covering the top with a circle of damp greaseproof paper to stop the skin from forming.
Separate the egg and beat the yolk into the cooled custard, then fold in the gooseberry purée. Whisk the egg white

stiffly. Whip the cream until thick and fold into the purée followed by the egg white. Add a few drops of green food colouring if liked. Pour into a container and freeze. When half frozen, whisk again until smooth. Return to the container, cover and freeze until firm. If frozen in a 500-ml (1-pint) pudding basin, the ice cream can be turned out like a 'bombe'.

This ice cream is fawn coloured. If you wish to colour it, do be very careful to use your colouring, literally one drop at a time.
Whipping cream is now on sale everywhere. It is so much easier to use than double cream, and seems to go further too.

PÊCHE MELBA

Serves 6

6 medium, ripe peaches
light sugar syrup (see page 33)
450 g (1 lb) raspberries, fresh or
    frozen
100 g (4 oz) icing sugar
575 ml (1 pint) vanilla ice cream
    (see page 85)

Skin the peaches by dipping them in boiling water. Lightly poach in a vanilla-flavoured light syrup. Drain, cool and chill. Rub the raspberries through a sieve and add the well sieved icing sugar to this purée.
Put the ice cream into a chilled glass dish or six individual glasses and cover it with halved peaches. Pour the raspberry purée, known all over the world as sauce melba, over the whole thing. Serve at once.

This is the famous dish created by Escoffier 'the King of cooks and cook of Kings' for Dame Nellie Melba. It is probably only at home that this lovely confection is properly made.

ORANGE SORBET

Serves 6

6 good-looking oranges
water or pure unsweetened orange
  juice
lemon juice
350 g (12 oz) granulated sugar
1 egg white
small bay leaves or mint leaves

Wash the oranges. Take a small circle right out of the top of each and a small slice off the base so they will 'sit'. Spoon out the insides into a bowl. Brush the raw edges with lemon juice. Put these cases into the freezer.

Sieve the orange flesh to extract all the juice. Make up to 850 ml (1½ pints) with water, or better still, pure unsweetened orange juice from a carton. Put the liquid with the sugar into a pan. Heat to melt the sugar completely then boil rapidly without stirring for 5 minutes. These measurements and timing are crucial. Take the pan off the heat, strain into a basin and leave to cool.

Whisk the egg white stiffly and fold into the mixture. Persevere with this. Pour into a suitable container and put into the coldest part of the freezer.

When firm, after maybe 3 hours, turn into a bowl and beat with an electric beater until smooth. This will give it the characteristic look of a sorbet. Bring out the oranges, and, working rapidly, spoon the sorbet into them, leaving a rough, piled top. Put the lids on at an angle with a bay leaf tucked in.

Put each orange into a polythene bag and put back into the freezer until wanted. They freeze very well, with no loss of colour so can be made in advance, *but* serve straight from the freezer to the table, without giving them time to melt.

Lemon sorbet can be made in exactly the same way, using lemons. A dish of lemon and orange sorbets served in fruit shells looks absolutely stunning.

TOM POUCE

Serves about 10

225 g (8 oz) pâte sucrée
  (see page 16)
100 g (4 oz) almonds,
  toasted
75 g (3 oz) butter, softneed
75 g (3 oz) caster sugar
1 tsp instant coffee powder (good
  quality)
coffee glacé icing (see page 73)

Heat the oven to 190°C (375°F) mark 5. Make the pastry, cover and leave to relax in the refrigerator while you make the crème noisette.

Put 75 g (3 oz) chopped nuts in a bowl and beat in the butter, sugar and the coffee powder.

Roll out the pastry and cut it into 5-cm (2-inch) squares. Put on to baking sheets lined with non-stick baking paper and cook for about 10 minutes or until honey coloured. Cool on a wire rack.

Sandwich very gently together in pairs with the crème noisette, allowing a little to show at the edges. Ice lightly with a coffee glacé icing and put a tiny sprinkling of the remaining chopped nuts in the middle. This is lovely with vanilla ice cream.

ORANGES IN CARAMEL

Serves 4–6

8 small oranges
850 ml (1½ pints) water
200 g (7 oz) granulated sugar
150-ml (¼-pint) carton orange juice

Peel the oranges and remove all traces of pith. Put them to simmer in the water with 25 g (1 oz) sugar for 10 minutes. Remove them, drain and put into a decorative dish.

Meanwhile, scrape or cut all the pith away from the peel of 2 oranges. Cut the peel into fine shreds, about 5 cm (2 inches) long. Dissolve 100 g (4 oz) granulated sugar in the orange juice, add the shreds and simmer steadily until the liquid becomes syrupy. Pour the syrup over the oranges, arranging the shreds on top.

Melt the remaining 50 g (2 oz) sugar in 2 tablespoons water. Boil rapidly without stirring to a warm honey colour. Pour over the oranges, rearranging a few shreds so they sit on top of the oranges. Serve chilled.

APRICOT CHANTILLY

Serves 4–6

450 g (1 lb) fresh apricots or dried
    apricots soaked overnight
grated rind and juice of 2 oranges
100 g (4 oz) granulated sugar
2 tbsp Cointreau
150 ml (¼ pint) whipping cream
25 g (1 oz) flaked almonds, toasted

Wash and stone the apricots. Drain if necessary. Simmer them together with the orange rind and juice gently adding a little water to cover. Stir in the sugar and melt over a low heat. Cool.

Purée in the blender or rub through a sieve, then add the Cointreau. Whip the cream until stiff and fold through the apricot purée. Serve in individual glasses with a few toasted almonds on top.

CREAM POSSET

Serves 4–6

2 medium lemons
275 ml (½ pint) whipping cream
50 ml (2 fl oz) dry white wine
2 tbsp caster sugar, approx
3 egg whites

Grate the rind and squeeze the juice of the lemons. Whip the cream until stiff and fold in the grated lemon rind. Stir in the lemon juice and the wine and about 2 tablespoons of sugar, or to taste.

Whisk the egg whites stiffly and fold into the creamy mixture. Serve in glasses.

POTS DE CHOCOLAT

Serves 6

175 g (6 oz) good dark chocolate
50 g (2 oz) butter, not margarine
2 eggs, separated
2 tbsp rum, or milk if preferred

Melt the chocolate in a basin over a pan of hot water. Remove from the heat. Cool a little then beat in the butter and the egg yolks followed by the rum or milk.

Whisk the egg whites very stiffly and fold into the chocolate mixture using a metal spoon. This will take quite a time, so gently persevere. Spoon into six small ramekins (which is the classic way to serve this) or into glasses (old-fashioned custard glasses look charming), and leave to set. Serve with tiny homemade macaroon or ratafia biscuits.

CHARLOTTE RUSSE

Serves 4

1 packet lemon jelly
glacé cherries
angelica
about 12 bought sponge fingers
275 ml (½ pint) milk
1 vanilla pod
15-g (½-oz) packet gelatine
3 egg yolks
25 g (1 oz) caster sugar
150 ml (¼ pint) whipping cream

Prepare a 750-ml (1½-pint) charlotte mould or soufflé dish. Make the jelly as directed on the packet. When cool, pour about 1 cm (½ inch) into the dish and chill until set. Decorate on top of the set jelly with a few cherries and angelica diamonds (this is important). Set another 1 cm (½ inch) of jelly. Leave the rest of the jelly to set.

Trim the bottom of the sponge fingers. Fit closely around the sides of the dish. The number needed will depend on the size of the dish.

Bring the milk to the boil with the vanilla pod. Dissolve the gelatine in 2 tablespoons of water in a bowl over hot water. Whisk the egg yolks and sugar until light and fluffy. Remove the vanilla pod and pour the hot milk over the eggs, beating all the time. Strain this custard into a bowl. Add the gelatine, pouring in a thin stream. Cool until just starting to set at the edges.

Whisk the cream lightly and fold into the custard with a metal spoon. Spoon at once into the charlotte case. Cover with foil and put into the refrigerator to set. When ready to serve, dip the dish into very hot water for a second or two. Turn out on to an attractive plate.

Chiffonade (chop) the remaining jelly and spoon around the base of the charlotte.

This is a famous 19th-century French dish.

Cover all milk and cream dishes in the refrigerator, otherwise they pick up the flavours of other foods around them.

LES CRÉMETS

Serves 4

2 egg whites
275 ml (½ pint) whipping cream
100 ml (4 fl oz) double cream
225–350 g (8–12 oz) strawberries
or raspberries or homemade
redcurrant or raspberry jelly

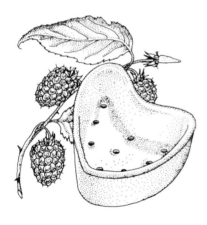

Whisk the egg whites and then whip the whipping cream until stiff. Fold the egg whites into the cream with a metal spoon.

Have ready four squares of fresh muslin. Fit them into four little heart-shaped moulds which have holes in the bottom. Spoon the cream into the moulds. Fold the muslin over. Stand on a rack to drain overnight if wanted at midday, or all day if wanted in the evening.

To serve, turn out on to individual pretty plates and cover completely with the unwhipped double cream. Serve with fresh strawberries or raspberries, or in the winter with a spoonful or so of homemade redcurrant or raspberry jelly.

The charming little dishes can be bought very reasonably at all good kitchen shops. Have all your equipment ready before starting. To save time, whisk egg whites before cream when using both, then you don't have to wash the beaters in between.

RASPBERRY FLUMMERY

Serves 4–6

225 g (8 oz) raspberries
50 g (2 oz) caster sugar
275 ml (½ pint) whipping cream
150 ml (¼ pint) sweet white wine

Look over and lightly bruise the raspberries. Leave a few whole. Sprinkle with 25 g (1 oz) sugar. Whip the cream stiffly. Fold in the remaining sugar and the wine. Fold the raspberries gently through and through the cream until it is striped with pink. Pile into sparkling glasses and decorate each with a whole raspberry or two. Serve chilled.

CHEESECAKE

Serves 6

50 g (2 oz) butter
100 g (4 oz) caster sugar
300 g (10 oz) cottage cheese
50 g (2 oz) ground almonds
50 g (2 oz) ground rice
50 g (2 oz) stoned raisins
1 lemon
2 eggs

Heat the oven to 180°C (350°F) mark 4. Grease a 23–25-cm (9–10-inch) loose-bottomed flan tin. Line the base with non-stick baking paper.

Cream the butter, sugar and cheese until white. Beat in the ground almonds and the ground rice and fold in the raisins. Grate the rind and squeeze the juice from the lemon. Separate the eggs. Beat the yolks into the mixture with the lemon rind and juice. Whisk the egg whites stiffly and fold evenly through the mixture. Cook for one hour, then cool and chill.

This is the classic cheesecake.

STRAWBERRY ROMANOFF

Serves 4–6

450 g (1 lb) strawberries
grated rind and juice of 1 orange
1 tbsp Grand Marnier
50 g (2 oz) caster sugar
150 ml (¼ pint) whipping cream

Cut the strawberries in half. Soak the fruit in the liqueur with the orange rind and juice and the sugar, reserving a teaspoon of sugar. Leave for an hour, or longer as convenient, giving a gentle stir from time to time.

When required, spoon the fruit carefully into a glass serving dish. Whip the cream with the remaining sugar, thus producing crème chantilly.

Pile on top of the strawberries and serve within an hour.

Fresh fruit, not canned, is required for this classic dish. Fresh ripe peaches or nectarines are lovely used in this way. Do not use more than 1 tablespoon of liqueur for a Romanoff, otherwise you will spoil it.

WHAT IS THE WI ?

If you have enjoyed this book, the chances are that you would enjoy belonging to the largest women's organisation in the country — the Women's Institutes.

We are friendly, go-ahead, like-minded women, who derive enormous satisfaction from all the movement has to offer. This list is long — you can make new friends, have fun and companionship, visit new places, develop new skills, take part in community services, fight local campaigns, become a WI market producer, and play an active role in an organisation which has a national voice.

The WI is the only women's organisation in the country which owns an adult education establishment. At Denman College, you can take a course in anything from car maintenance to paper sculpture, from book binding to yoga, or cordon bleu cookery to fly-fishing.

All you need to do to join is write to us here at the **National Federation of Women's Institutes, 39 Eccleston Street, London SW1W 9NT**, or telephone 01-730 7212, and we will put you in touch with WIs in your immediate locality. We hope to hear from you.

ABOUT THE AUTHOR

Janet Wier is a City and Guilds trained cookery teacher and taught the cake icing and sweet-making courses at the WI's Denman College for several years. She is a WI National Cookery Judge, Demonstrator and Assessor. She belongs to Bramshaw WI, is a past County Chairman and Voluntary County Market Organiser of Hampshire. Other books by the author include *Can She Cook?*, *Cook — Yes She Can* and *Cooking for the Family*.

INDEX